MASTERING OFFICE POLITICS

Learn the fine points of office politics including:

- Making points with a new boss
- The art of dealing with criticism
- Working with your hotshot assistant
- Taking a temporary step down
- How to turn tension and conflict into action
- The art of motivating employees
- Three ways to gain allies in your company
- Racial conflicts on the job
- Getting the message across under fire
- Helping employees through personal crises
- When to say "I'm the boss!"
- Surviving when your company is merged
- Being an outsider in your own company
- Job-hunting strategies for managers over 50
- Handling the hostile employee
- Making room for the promising rookie
- Living with the whistle-blower
- AND MUCH MORE!

***Don't miss the next book
in the series
from the
National Institute of Business Management:***

MASTERING DECISION MAKING

THE TOTAL MANAGEMENT PROGRAM FOR THE 1990s!
From the National Institute of Business Management

THIS REMARKABLE NEW SERIES INCLUDES:

MASTERING MEETINGS
MASTERING OFFICE POLITICS
MASTERING DECISION MAKING
MASTERING BUSINESS WRITING
MASTERING BUSINESS STYLE

THE ESSENTIAL KEYS TO SUCCESS FOR TODAY'S MANAGERS

Coming soon from Berkley Books

MASTERING OFFICE POLITICS

HOW TO FINESSE YOUR WAY TO SUCCESS

National Institute of Business Management

BERKLEY BOOKS, NEW YORK

This Berkley book contains the complete text
of the original edition. It has been
completely reset in a typeface designed for easy
reading and was printed from new film.

MASTERING OFFICE POLITICS

A Berkley Book / published by arrangement with
National Institute of Business Management, Inc.

PRINTING HISTORY
National Institute of Business Management, Inc.,
edition / January 1989
Berkley trade paperback edition / February 1991

ISBN: 0-425-12560-2

A BERKLEY BOOK® TM 757,375
Berkley Books are published by The Berkley Publishing Group,
200 Madison Avenue, New York, New York 10016.
The name "Berkley" and the "B" logo
are trademarks belonging to Berkley Publishing Corporation.

PRINTED IN THE UNITED STATES OF AMERICA

10 9 8 7 6 5 4 3 2 1

INTRODUCTION

Like it or not, every day you do battle in a hard-knocks world called "work." No matter what you do for a living, or where you fit into the organization, you can reach your goal faster, get along better, and succeed sooner if you have the right management techniques. That means managing those you work *for* as well as those who work *for you*. These are not difficult things—mostly common sense—really. But this book will remind you of what you need to do to succeed in the office, and it will refresh your memory on the "right" way to get ahead.

Office politics is a fact of life. It doesn't mean "dirty tricks" or Machiavellian maneuvering. It means:

— using your inherent charm to get people to do what you want them to do,
— leading people in a way that cultivates respect,
— getting the job done and getting it done well, and
— making sure those above you see what you have accomplished.

It also means reaping the rewards of your hard work.

This book is divided into five major sections representing the most important components of a successful career—**The Politics of Advancement, The Politics of Teamwork, The Politics of Leadership, The Politics of Change,** and **Managing Difficult Employees.** Within these sections is practical advice the Institute has compiled from interviews with hundreds of managers just like you.

Read in its entirety, this book will tell you how to recognize and seize opportunities to advance your career, position, and salary by working *with* people, not for or against them. It is also structured to be a "Manager's First Aid" handbook. When you are in a situation that troubles you or you have an employee who is not working up to your standards—see how others handled it. There are more than 80 situations outlined here; look through the Table of Contents to see which ones fit your needs.

Refer to this book often during the next several weeks, and you will have finished a crash course in managing your career that you can't get at any university.

TABLE OF CONTENTS

Section I
The Politics of Advancement

Section II
The Politics of Teamwork

Section III
The Politics of Leadership

Section IV
The Politics of Change

Section V
Managing Difficult Employees

THE POLITICS OF ADVANCEMENT

Going Over Your Boss's Head

If your career is temporarily stalled because your boss is in your way, you're faced with three options: You can grin and bear it, quit, or take the bull by the horns and go over your boss's head.

What kinds of situations might provoke taking such drastic action?

— **Not being acknowledged.** Each time you complete an important project, your boss takes most of the credit in order to score points with his boss.

— **Incompetent behavior.** Your boss knows practically nothing about running a department or your industry. His or her only qualification was being the child or friend of a high-ranking executive.

— **Tyrannical behavior.** Your boss runs the department using terror tactics. This person makes unreasonable demands ("I expect you to come in over the weekend to complete this report") and verbally assaults everyone who reports to him ("If our sales goal isn't reached, forget about getting a good performance appraisal and expect a memo to be sent to the president").

— **Sexual harassment.** Your work is exemplary, and yet you haven't received a raise or promotion in 18 months because you've shunned your boss's sexual advances.

How should you proceed? Very cautiously, insists Dr. Charles Grothe, co-author with Dr. Peter Wylie of *Problem Bosses* (Facts on File, 460 Park Ave. So., New York, NY 10016; $19.95). He offers these pointers:

▪ **Examine the situation closely.** What kind of person is your boss's boss? Can you present your case, and will the information be objectively and maturely weighed? This person may be no different from your boss, or the two of them may be best friends. In either case, you are doomed before you start.

- **How is your performance record?** If you're a star performer with an impressive track record, you stand a better chance of achieving your ends. If you're marginal (and expendable), senior managers may not want to go out on a limb for you.

What Not to Do

Don't act impulsively. Don't stomp into anyone's office and vent your frustrations in an emotional tirade. This will do more harm than good in the end because you really won't be rational enough to make a very convincing case for yourself.

Here's a Strategy

- **Decide which boss to approach.** If your boss's boss is unapproachable, move up the ladder until you find the best person. In small companies, for example, the ideal person may be the president.

- **Prepare for your meeting.** Think of yourself as a prosecutor gathering evidence before taking a case to court. Gather relevant material for your presentation that would support your contentions. *Examples:* evidence that a performance appraisal hasn't been written in two years; documentation that your boss wouldn't stand behind good ideas; dated memos outlining cost-cutting suggestions that were ignored.

- **Stick to facts and issues.** Instead of just outlining the problem areas, offer specific solutions. *Example:* If you're stalemated because your boss won't support new projects, demonstrate that they're feasible and what they would mean to the bottom line.

- ■ **Observation:** Be aware that bypassing your boss can lead to resentment—overt or hidden. You could risk your job in this kind of maneuver.

  "Going over your boss's head to report abusive, unfair or unjust treatment is not squealing or ratting," asserts Grothe. "On the contrary, it's an act of courage and responsibility more managers should be willing to carry out. If they did, it would dramatically

4

reduce the number of bosses who flagrantly abuse their power.''
In short, it can become a moral obligation.

Living With a Domineering Boss

It's not unusual to find that otherwise normal people become virtually unbearable when they're given a title and responsibility. They put so much effort into maintaining control that they become oppressive.

Take Ted Carmine's situation, for example. Carmine is a new unit manager who reports to the director of operations. It's a job with a lot of promise, or it would be if it weren't for Walter Baggot, his boss. Baggot tries to rule with an iron hand. He brooks no opposition, makes arbitrary decisions, takes offense if anyone in his group stands out. He's got the position, the authority and the power—and you had better not forget it.

This makes tough going for the people who report to him. Carmine has already had any number of run-ins with Baggot over ideas, proposals, rules and procedures, but he wants to stick it out, if at all possible—the potential for advancement within the organization is great. He does wonder, though, whether there isn't some possible way to ease the strain.

One big obstacle in dealing with this type of boss is the hope that you will be able to change the person's outlook with rational argument. But that's not likely to happen, at least in any major way. It's more practical, therefore, not to take a crusader's attitude, but rather, to find ways to improve the relationship by making a personal adaptation. Here's how you might go about it:

- **Figure out whom you're dealing with.** Obviously, there is an underlying reason for your boss's domineering behavior. It may be a reaction to a tough climb up the organizational ladder, or it may be a strategy developed to cope with undue pressure. It may simply be a cover-up for basic insecurity. Whatever the cause, this is the way your boss is—and will probably continue to be.

    If you face this fact squarely and anticipate the kind of behavior you are likely to encounter in a given situation, you can take some

5

of the pressure off yourself. An attitude of "There he goes again" can help you shrug off some of the incidents that you now seem to find so maddening.

- **Pick a judicious course.** Certainly, you don't want to play the toady—meekly accepting every whim and arbitrary decision made by your boss in an attempt to please. That would make it too difficult to live with yourself. Nor would you want to go to the opposite extreme—open resistance. There are too many ways an angry boss can do you in. Your best bet, in most cases, is to take the middle path—maintaining your independence by making a strategic fight for those things you consider important while, at the same time, going along with boss-imposed ideas or procedures that may be distasteful but can't adversely affect your operation.

- **Keep your distance.** This may not always be possible since domineering bosses like close control. But there are strategies you can use to cope. One manager advises "Learn to do everything right the first time around. There are no problems, then, to attract your boss's attention." Another manager recommends building a network of information sources. "That way," she says, "you can cut down substantially on the number of times you have to seek your boss's assistance."

  While maintaining distance, however, don't let yourself be overshadowed by your boss's behavior. Make contacts, forge alliances, become highly visible in other areas of the organization. Just be careful that you don't downgrade your boss while you're doing this. Others may be happy to repeat what you've told them—to your boss.

- **Learn as much as possible.** A boss who is domineering may still be able to teach you a great deal. He or she may be highly creative or an expert in your field. A sincere interest then, in how this person does it, could mark the start of a more comfortable relationship.

  Equally true, you can learn what not to do, how not to act. If your boss takes credit for your ideas, for instance, or never praises the good work you do, you know how this tends to discourage and demotivate you. Knowledge of this kind can be extremely helpful in your dealings with others—at the present time and in the future as well.

- - **Observation:** It's comforting to realize that no boss is forever. Eventually, you will come to a parting of the ways. When that time comes, you will be in a good position to forge ahead, having proved to yourself and to others that you could meet a challenge— and that you have the ability to learn from it when it becomes necessary.

Distance Yourself
From a Boss in Trouble

When Ray Perkins resigned as head coach of the New York Giants, he took over as coach at the University of Alabama, where he once played on the team. "It's been a dream of mine for a long time," he later explained to reporters at a press conference.

To team owners, players and fans, his leave-taking came as a surprise. But there was one group—the offensive and defensive coaches of the team—to whom it came as a real jolt. The new head coach made it quite clear that he regarded them as Ray Perkins' men—and that he wanted to choose his own staff. Chances were, therefore, that not many of them would be with the Giants during the next season.

Similar situations occur in many organizations. An executive whose star is on the rise gathers together a group of his or her own choosing. They work closely and well as a cadre for a certain period of time. When the executive's star goes out—things haven't worked out as expected, or he or she leaves for greener pastures—the cadre members are left without a leader and sometimes with no place to go. They are so closely identified with one person that others hesitate to take them on.

At some point in your career, you may find yourself joining just such a group. You find the atmosphere challenging and exciting, the esprit de corps refreshing, and that is as it should be. But you would do well to keep yourself and your own career in mind—and observe certain cautions. For example . . .

- **Don't wear a name tag**—or at least one that shouts "I belong to Joe X." Some people are so quick to identify themselves as part of "Joe's team" that their own names get lost in the shuffle. It's better to come across as an individual in your own right who happens to be working in a particular area, on a particular project. Talk about what you're doing, sure, but make it your job and your work.

- **Be leery of oversocializing.** In many cases, people in a team atmosphere seize every opportunity to "huddle" with the head coach. Coffee breaks, afternoon chats, long lunches, drinks after work—all are used to develop closer ties to the top. The end result is, though, that these people become more and more identified with the leader, not only on a business basis but also on a social one.

  A certain amount of socializing is fine—but be judicious.

- **Develop a wide range of contacts.** The more people you know, the more people who know about you and the work you are doing, the better your chances are of continuing in your career, should your manager leave. So get to know people in all areas of the organization—share your thinking, show interest in what they do, discuss mutual problems and triumphs. If and when the day comes that the boss leaves, the knowledge others have of you, as a professional and a person, will stand you in good stead.

- **Gain visibility in your own right.** Volunteer to lead a series of planning meetings or head a community fundraising campaign. Make a speech to the sales force. Write an article for a management periodical and/or for your own house organ. The more light you shine on yourself, the more attention you receive as an individual, the better your chances are of demonstrating your own capabilities, skill and potential.

- - **Observation:** It can be both challenging and rewarding to work with a top-notch person. But it may not last forever. You can prepare for that eventuality by working hard for the team while maintaining your own identity and preparing for an uncertain future at the same time.

How to Disagree With Your Boss

A good manager knows when it is time to disagree with the boss, says career consultant John Crystal.

Differing on policy, procedure or even questioning an order is highly recommended, he says. "Most bosses welcome intelligent disagreement. They respect aggressive workers who have the courage to contradict and ask questions. That's one way to move up the corporate ladder."

What's important, he stresses, is knowing *how to do it*. "Like extracting an elephant's tooth, do it very carefully," advises Crystal. Ask yourself:

- **Is this issue worth disagreeing on?** What will you gain? Are you just disagreeing or do you staunchly believe you're right? Are your principles being violated? Is it a procedural difference of opinion or is it a moral or ethical question?

- **What alternatives can I offer?** "If you're going to take a stand, have solid reasons behind it or an unbeatable argument in your defense," says Crystal.

  When you articulate your opinions:

- **Avoid anger.** Getting angry is a waste of time. If there is an open display of hostility between junior and senior, the junior staff member always loses.

- **Reverse roles.** Before voicing objections, put yourself in your boss's shoes. What would you do in his or her place? How would you respond to a dissenting opinion? Might you see things differently if you were boss?

- **Understand your superior's personality.** How is he or she going to react? Will it be a rational (reflective and considerate) or an emotional (possible volatile) response?

- **Be tactful.** Be direct, but diplomatic if you can. Sometimes open disagreement may not be the best course of action, Crystal explains further. Try expressing your opinion in the form of a question.

9

Example: "How do you think the vice president of operations will feel about the change?"

You are asking your boss to question whether or not the change will be approved by his or her superior. "By employing this round-about strategy, you're creating a platform for your own views," says Crystal.

■■ **Observation:** If you have a difficult boss who doesn't want to discuss differences, Crystal suggests expressing your dissent in writing and keeping a copy for yourself. "If there is evidence to support your opposing views, a new manager may disassociate you from your ex-boss and his or her mistakes," says Crystal.

Making Points With a New Boss

The reorganization is over and you have a new boss. It's been a chaotic few months. But the dust is settling and it's time to get on with business as usual. You may hold the same job, but this new person represents a towering question mark and source of uncertainty. How do you make this new relationship work? Richard Gould, author of *Sacked* (John Wiley Sons, 1 Wiley Dr., Somerset, NJ 08873; $18.95) offers these suggestions:

■ **Change your perception of your job.** Look upon it as a new job. Your functions and title may be the same, but all your former power relationships must be reassessed. The way you will be doing your job, along with how and when you're supervised, will be different. No matter what kind of record you have, you can't expect past performance to make points with your new boss. A more realistic attitude is to assume that you're starting with a clean slate.

■ **Size him or her up.** Do this immediately. Your first few days together can tell you a lot. Study your boss's work methods. Do some research. What kind of company did this person work for before? Was it rigid and bureaucratic or freewheeling? Watch how decisions are made. How does this boss treat people? Is the individual distant and cold or friendly and outgoing?

Compare yourself to this person. What are the similarities and differences? Could these differences pose a problem? Can anything be done about them? How can these differences complement each other? *Example:* You're very energetic and your boss is laid back and easygoing. You enjoy making quick decisions, but your boss prefers to think things over and consider them carefully. Or, if you're creative and imaginative and she lacks these skills, you can be of great value.

- **Communication is vital.** It's easy if your boss is outgoing, but very difficult if he or she is introverted and suspicious. Typically, the boss determines what kind of communication exists. If the person is a noncommunicator, it's up to you to keep the channels open by making sure there is a lot of contact.

- **Offer assistance.** Put yourself in this person's place. It's a new job, in a new setting, complicated by new faces. Offer as much help as you can. *Example:* Introduce her to people she needs to know—the benefits expert, purchasing manager, office personnel who process expense forms. Give her some insights into the corporate culture.

- **Take the initiative to keep the relationship from going off track.** If you feel it's not what you'd like it to be, don't wait for her to fix it. You do it. Don't sit on a misunderstanding. Move in and take action so it's corrected. *Example:* "I'd like to clarify and elaborate on a point I made at the luncheon meeting. I don't want you to misunderstand what I said about revamping the West Coast sales strategy you set up."

- **Be prepared for some rough times.** The relationship is not going to click into place immediately. It will take time, a few months at least.

- **Be objective and realistic about the viability of the relationship.** If it's not working, find a way out. Don't be naive and think all situations can be rectified. Your work styles may be dissimilar, or your philosophy and ideas too far apart, or the chemistry may just be all wrong. If this is the case, update your résumé and scour the marketplace.

11

When You Socialize With Your Boss

Your boss has asked you to lunch, dinner or a weekend golf game. If it's the first time or a rare event, you may feel anxious because you're unsure what the purpose is or how to act. But if handled correctly, these occasions can help you develop a stronger working relationship with your boss. Here's what to keep in mind:

- **Take cues from your boss.** If your boss keeps business out of the conversation, it's risky for you to mention office matters. If you're unsure whether something is appropriate, refer to it briefly and watch the reaction. Nonverbal behavior (sitting back, looking away) can be a clue that your boss doesn't feel comfortable talking about the subject. So can a verbal response—a humorous comment rather than a question.

- **Drink in moderation**—or not at all. Even if a few drinks don't normally affect you, it's smart to stick to a wine spritzer or a beer if you feel it's appropriate because your boss is drinking. Drinking more isn't worth the risk of saying or doing something you'll later regret.

- **Avoid revealing personal information.** No matter what your boss chooses to tell you about his or her personal affairs, it's not smart to talk about your marital, family, financial or health problems. Nor is it advisable to betray any lack of confidence about your professional abilities, your career choice or your job. What your boss doesn't know really can't hurt you.

- **Be cautious in your comments about other staff members.** If you're asked your opinion of other employees or what you know about them personally, don't be overly critical or supply too many details. Instead, try to address your boss's concern and offer suggestions on how the problem or situation could be remedied. If, for example, you're asked whether you've noticed that a colleague has a drinking problem, talk about ways the person might be helped rather than focusing on the times he or she has been late or botched an assignment.

- **Keep the socializing "professional" if your boss is of the opposite sex.** The more relaxed the setting, the more opportunity there is for misinterpretation of language and behavior. Individuals who suspect their boss's intention may be romantic or sexual are smart to bring up their spouses, "significant others" or family if the conversation takes such a turn.

- **Don't confuse your role as a subordinate with your role as a friend.** Even if you and your boss become buddies, you shouldn't lose sight of the fact that your boss still has power over your job and your paycheck. And if you expect special consideration because you're a friend, you're setting yourself up for disappointment.

- ▪ **Recommendation:** If your boss invites you more often than your colleagues, don't advertise that fact. Your colleagues may be reluctant to share information or work closely with you if they feel you have access to the boss that they don't.

Living With a Low-Feedback Boss

"How do you think it went?" Clem's boss, John Graves, asked him as they left the meeting. Clem replied in detail, as John smiled, nodded, and interjected "um-hum's" and "very interesting's" at appropriate points. Mulling over the incident much later, Clem realized that, as usual, he had no idea what Graves thought.

If you have a tight-lipped, uncommunicative boss, you know how frustrating and annoying it can be. The difficult part is that you really can't dislike this person—he or she is never unpleasant and does genuinely seem to want to know what you are thinking. Ideally, you'd like there to be some give-and-take to the confidences. And yet there can be some advantages to this type of situation:

- You may have more autonomy than you realize. Since you don't know what your boss is thinking, you can take chances, try things without deliberately defying him or her.

13

- You probably enjoy more leeway in how you run your own work group and in the way you deal with your employees than you would under a boss whose opinions were usually stated openly.

- You may have an opportunity to establish close relationships with fellow managers. Since you are all in the same uncharted waters, it pays to support each other.

But if these benefits do not outweigh the disadvantages, and you still wish you knew what the boss is thinking, there are some strategies to consider:

- **Look for patterns.** Although people are not always consistent, a review of your boss's past decisions can give you some pattern for predicting future behavior.

- **Put it in writing.** What about jotting down your evaluations and asking for comments? Some people can respond more easily in writing than orally.

- **Try your own waiting game.** Next time your boss asks your opinion, try responding noncommittally—or minimally. Create some silence, and he or she may surprise you by filling it up.

- **Be persistent and ask questions.** "What do you think?"—asked often enough—just might get you a response. The boss may not be aware that there is a lack of information-sharing, and can be prodded to change. Or you might become specific and offer a practical reason as to why you need to know what he or she is thinking.

- **Observation:** There is no simple solution to this particular problem. Maybe none of these strategies will give you all the information you need. But they may provide just enough to make your work easier and give you a more secure feeling in this uncomfortable situation.

When You're Faced
With Bypassing Your Boss

Going over your boss's head is a dangerous political play, and you should know the stakes before you start. You might carry it off, but if you don't, the damage to your career can be far-reaching, and your recourse limited. In fact, in a recent court case, a large oil company's dismissal of a manager was upheld as legitimate because he had repeatedly ignored the chain of command by going over his superiors' heads.

As one behaviorist puts it, "Deliberately or blatantly going over or around your immediate superior can make you appear dangerous to organizational order and morale. It can make you suspect among your peers, put you at permanent odds with your superior, and cause you to be seen as a troublemaker by higher management."

But what if your boss is an obstacle, a pain in the neck? Well, you can take alternative courses to further your own ends:

- **Break what you want into bite-sized pieces.** If, for example, you want to implement a new system, but your boss instinctively fends off change of this magnitude, don't present it as a system. Instead, break up your idea into small alterations of present practices. Making changes—gradually—will also help others to get used to them. And your boss may ease into acceptance rather than fight against them.

- **Volunteer to help out.** If your boss is excessively busy, the more receptive he or she might be to the idea of letting you go ahead on some matters on your own. You might even get the boss to agree to your consulting with higher-ups as your boss's emissary—if you take pains to keep him or her continuously posted on what you're doing.

- **Draw higher-ups into the picture.** If your boss has trouble making decisions or is removed from the power centers, you might suggest meetings on issues of concern to you that include—along with your boss—others within or outside of the organization with an interest in the matter. If you promote such a meeting as a tool for information-gathering, for idea exchange, for sounding out others' thoughts on the matter, it will not appear as a threat to your boss's status but, rather, as a boost and therefore acceptable. Then, when you are at these meetings, you will be able to tell what kind of support you can expect for your project.

- **Work through others** if you want results more than you want the credit. In a case where you want to get something done, but your boss is overtly opposed, seek out other organizational channels through which the same idea could be implemented. Let someone else, who may be grateful for the idea you're offering run with your ball. Extra benefit: He or she may want to reciprocate.

- **Keep your files current** on projects or ideas you advance and which are stymied by your boss's resistance or inaction. You never know when times and circumstances will change, making your idea excitingly relevant. By keeping track of what you have done, if an opening does develop, you'll be ready.

- ▪ **Observation:** The chain of command isn't inviolate, and there may come a time when you feel you have to break it. If so, be careful, and prepare yourself for the worst.

What if Your Boss Shoots Down All Your New Ideas?

"Dear Sirs/Ladies:" writes a Kansas manager, *"I'm getting frustrated. Ideas, suggestions or complaints do not make it past my boss—the production manager of this bank that services 33 correspondent banks. I am in charge of the second shift, which has 14 people doing heavy data processing production work. There are good people working here, but whenever I bring up a problem or complaint from someone on my shift or the night shift, he usually says, 'Maybe it will go away.' About the only thing that moves him to some action is when his boss, a Senior VP, hears about a problem and directs him to take some action.*

"As for ideas or suggestions, he doesn't want to be bothered. He seems to care nothing for employees' feelings or needs. I become the

middle man (actually I'm a woman), trying to explain why their ideas got shot down, or why they have to contend with problems left by other shifts. In this situation, it's difficult to explain to those I manage why they should keep their attitude toward the company positive. It's also difficult to deal with this kind of boss. What would you advise me to do?''

There are, unfortunately, managers in key positions who want little or nothing to do with the overall responsibility they are paid to fulfill. They see their jobs as simply ''running a smooth operation.'' They don't want to hear about new directions, innovations or needed modifications. And those who continue to come to them with suggestions of this kind may acquire, in their boss's mind, the reputation of being troublemakers. If this is the way it is with your boss, and you find it too stupefying to knuckle under, then here are some actions you might consider:

- **Maybe you can go it on your own.** There are times, depending on the personalities involved, when a manager can take unilateral action without disturbing a passive boss. One manager, for instance, awarded days off to employees who contributed useable productivity ideas to her unit without consulting her boss. A problem with this ''unauthorized'' approach, however, is that it can leave you— and perhaps your staff—vulnerable to criticism from a boss who may hear of what you're doing from sources other than yourself, and become leery about what you may decide to do next. On the other hand . . .

- **Your success could increase your stature.** Unilateral actions become less easy to criticize when they are obviously the product of good judgment and bring good results. Let's say you can solve problems by conferring with other managers on your level rather than seeking action through your do-nothing boss. True, your boss may feel threatened in this circumstance, and you may have some explaining to do. On the other hand, if your approach is one that has been to every one's advantage, then the respect and recognition you may have gained in the organization could immunize you against criticism from a boss who is not respected. But if going this far isn't enough . . .

- **Try to cultivate your boss's boss.** Winning support from the person to whom your boss reports may be the final step you'll have to take to solidify your own position within the firm. It's possible that the

17

previous steps—working on your own, peer support—have already gained you credibility in this direction. In fact, this could be so even if some of the comments made about you have been negatively intended (''She's always pushing for something else,'' or ''He never knows how to let well enough alone''). Your boss's boss may welcome this kind of drive and determination in one of the company's employees.

But rather than wait for such recognition, why not actually promote it on your own? You can seek as much contact as possible with the person over your boss, so that he or she has the chance to know you, and to understand what you're trying to accomplish. True, such contact may be construed as bypassing—and this is dangerous when your boss is active and respected, but not so dangerous otherwise. If you have a boss who offers no help, no solutions, no interest, no encouragement, then you have to go to someone who can respond. If your boss's boss is where you must finally go for this kind of organizational assistance, then your need will probably be recognized and your actions countenanced.

▪ ▪ **Observation:** Hierarchies and tables of organization exist for a rational reason—they promote accountability and help organizations run in a systematic, and thus, effective fashion. But when inactive managers occupy key positions, the system tends to become unresponsive and quite stagnant as well. In such a circumstance, a lower level manager does the organization a definite service in doing what an inactive boss should have done, and this should certainly be recognized by the company.

When a Consultant Studies Your Operation

Ever since disciples of efficiency expert Frederick Taylor began lurking around factories with stop-watches, independent consultants have been increasingly influential and numerous. During the past several years more top M.B.A. grads have gone into management consulting than into any other field. So, as a manager, the odds are you'll eventually find yourself being examined by one of these corporate healers.

18

It may be unexpected. Certainly, when undertaking a large consulting project, the organization ought to involve its managers from the beginning. But sometimes, top management muddles internal communications and middle management concerns are steamrolled. Suddenly your operation's due for a checkup and it's up to you to make sure that you come out of it looking good, feeling good and gainfully employed. Here are some strategic observations and suggestions toward reaching that end:

- **Neither resist nor ignore what's happening.** Upper management has hired a consultant, and you'd better find out why. Management may be thinking of altering your operation or eliminating some jobs—including yours. This may be due to new executive policy, marketing strategy or the availability of new technology, rather than how well you've been doing your job. But you'll still be affected.

- **You have a right to question an outsider's ability to judge your operation.** While consultants claim specialized expertise, the benefit of other companies' experience and the perspective to look at the whole picture, an internal approach might work better. Perhaps you can negotiate. You may agree, for example, that management's plan to hire EDP consultants to install word processors would save money, but fear that management intends to fire people. By negotiating, you may be able to arrange for retraining and transfers, thus helping your staff through the transition.

- **Accept any opportunity to act as liaison with the consultant.** This could enable you to clarify the mission, spell out the boundaries of the project and the nature of the relationship. You may find that time and money are being spent in the wrong way. For instance, one company hired a consultant to help with reorganization and wound up with 100 pages of recommendations rather than the hands-on implementation it expected. Another discovered that its marketing consultant had plans to interview customers, when all the company expected was an analysis of its internal operations.

- **Identify the consultant's role.** A team of experts from a major consulting firm may be studying allocation of resources and mapping five-year strategy. They will come in as analytical and diagnostic specialists whose main interest is in providing answers to top management on planning and policy questions, perhaps to establish new methods or structures. On the other hand, process-oriented consultants—the organizational resources, human resources development, behavioral science types—will work to facilitate organizational change.

The difference in approaches is sometimes explained this way: You can hire someone to think for you or someone to help you think for yourself. In either case, when consultants come knocking on your door for an interview, it's a good idea to know how they perceive their role before you begin revealing yourself.

- **Consultants like openness,** but be careful when talking about people and departments. As a manager, your main contact with consultants is apt to be in providing information and insights. They will be examining how the system operates, looking for tensions and opportunities for improvement. It pays to play it straight, because you can't hide real problems from an experienced eye. But as you get rolling, keep some perspective. Talk in terms of organizational issues, not personalities. Talk about communications with purchasing, not about "that idiot over in purchasing." If you attack someone, particularly your boss, it may come back to haunt you.

- **Don't blame others for your problems;** take responsibility for your own function. If there is a problem in your area, make it clear that you are aware of it and want to work on it. If you complain that your employees are ineffective, your co-workers uncooperative, it mainly will reflect on you. Even if some of your complaints are true, you'll look professional if you take leadership responsibility and a problem-solving approach.

- **Volunteer to implement consultant recommendations,** so that you can make them workable. Thus, if a consultant brought in to do a survey of employee attitudes on safety goes directly to your supervisors and hourly workers, don't sit and stew thinking, "We'll see how far he gets without me." Speak with your boss or the consultants and suggest that you have some insights to bring to the problem.

- **Don't just roll over submissively.** Studies, recommendations and implementation take time. If you're perceptive about what's happening and feel your interests are under assault, you can act. Interview the consultants about their objectives and observations. Don't let their consultants' report be the only factor. Document your situation: your goals, needs and problems; what your people are doing; the progress you've made; the value of your operation. Get whatever help you can from those who are your friends—found in high places.

■ ■ **Observation** If you have to defend yourself, focus on the work, on the best way of getting the job done. Try to protect your people, your operation, and ultimately yourself, while at the same time demonstrating that you're a team player who understands company objectives. However, if the situation looks unsalvageable, examine your other options, gather support and begin to prepare a job search early. Don't be caught off guard by that pink slip if and when it comes, because you will be the loser.

Survival Skills
for the '90s and Beyond

Being primed and ready for the unexpected has always been a valuable talent. In today's turbulent business environment, where mergers, acquisitions and reorganizations are changing the face of American business, managers need that adaptability more than ever. What are the skills that allow good managers to respond readily to change? There are five principal ones:

1. **Problem-solving ability.** Because we're a global economy dominated by multinational companies, problems are appearing much more quickly and they are more severe than they were before. There is a lot of ambiguity and there are many paradoxes. Along with polished business smarts, you must also be problem-smart. Your antennae must detect problems early and be sensitive to potential difficulties before anyone else's. Your intuitive powers must be razor-sharp so you can detect a problem's early warning signals. Once found, you can determine the appropriate solution.
   Example: BankAmerica built expensive banks all over California. As the company expanded, the ground collapsed from under it because it was unable to anticipate problems early. For

example, it was slow to pick up on automated banking systems. To grow rapidly, the bank doubled agricultural lending and added $9 billion of foreign loans and $8 billion of fixed-rate mortgage loans. The strategy backfired by eventually producing huge loan losses and an accompanying interest rate squeeze that proved painful.

2. **Interpersonal understanding.** Know how to work with people and get things done through them. Be able to identify the other person's objectives and find viable ways to realize them. Step into the other person's shoes so that you can understand the individual's objectives and offer practical solutions for realizing them.

   Example: People Express' Donald Burr developed the idea of airbuses. Instead of designing a product (airline) to suit his customer's needs, Burr designed his product so customers would conform to the airline's standards. People Express offered cheap fares and nothing else. The concept worked well for about a year and a half before travelers stopped putting up with constant delays, erratic treatment or service and crowded travel accommodations.

   Structurally, the company was a disaster. It had a minimal bureaucracy, an inefficient deployment of workers, and a disorganized chain of command. Tack on an unstable airline industry picture, and it was no wonder Burr was unable to use his people productively. When you're in a volatile environment, discipline within the ranks is crucial. If you have no clear leadership in such crises, workers flounder and the operation falters.

3. **Analytical powers.** Good managers must be able to understand complex subjects and reduce them to manageable essentials. There is only a handful of solutions to any complex problem. A balance sheet, for example, contains an overwhelming amount of information. But when you establish your objectives, the numbers become a lot clearer and you can zero in on the essential ones that tell you what you need to know. There is a great deal of information available to managers, making it expedient to know how to access, interpret and analyze the most important facts that each situation demands.

   Example: Thornton Bradshaw had his hands full when he assumed the helm as CEO of a dangerously listing RCA in 1981. The company was in a state of chaos and decline. Within six years, four chief executives and a roundtable of presidents and

22

subsidiary heads came and went with no sign of stability on the horizon. Profits plummeted by 83%. Bradshaw analyzed the mammoth company and isolated the core businesses, which were entertainment (NBC) and consumer and military electronics. Everything else (Hertz Rent-A-Car and CIT Financial, for example) was deemed extraneous.

The diversified company lacked identity. Bradshaw put RCA back on track by trimming unnecessary fat, streamlining the operating companies, and enhancing those operations that could restore it to a leadership position. When the company was finally turned around, Bradshaw sold it to General Electric, a brilliant, calculated maneuver.

4. **Sensitivity to change.** Change is inescapable in today's shifting business environment. The idea is not just to be flexible and adaptable so you can adjust to it, but to anticipate change. The attitude shouldn't be, "How do we get the thing organized so that we can deal with what's going on?" but, "How will we make this thing go when what's going on changes?"

   Example: USX, the nation's largest steel producer had to cut its white collar work force by nearly 60% between 1982 and 1986. Management watched the change taking place in the steel industry, but did little to cushion itself against a dwindling market.

5. **Composure under pressure.** When things get hot, you must keep cool. There is no secret remedy for success. High-functioning managers cope with stress in a number of ways. They jog, swim, bike, play racquetball or golf, meditate and listen to music. It doesn't matter what escape valve you use. If it relieves tension, continue to use it. But even with tension-relieving techniques, it pays to be a little on edge, a trifle nervous. A little burr under your saddle helps you sprint into action when an emergency strikes.

   Example: When the airline industry was hit with an air traffic controllers strike in 1983, Drew Lewis (now president and COO of Union Pacific Corporation), then Secretary of Transportation, kept his cool when the controllers lost their perspective. He fired all the controllers, broke the union and was hailed as a hero. Despite the strike, he kept the airlines running. He kept his emotions in check, remained calm and in control, and acted rationally as well.

23

A Division Manager's Survival Guide

You've just been offered a plum post as manager of a large division in an international corporation. Before uncorking the champagne and calling all your friends with the news, consider:

Ideally, managers of decentralized operations are expected to act like autonomous, free-ranging, market-sensitive executives—much like the classic entrepreneur. But in reality, you are often trapped in a hierarchical middle, held accountable for profit-center responsibility while, at the same time, chief executive officers and their surrogates violate your autonomy without recognizing it, sometimes even going behind your back to intervene on divisional turf.

If you are offered a division manager's job, talk to the CEO (it will be the chief operating officer in a very large corporation) and ask, ''What kinds of decisions do you see yourself getting involved in?''

How does the answer correspond with your expectations regarding autonomy? Can you live with it?

One rule of thumb regarding a reasonable, appropriate breakdown of responsibility goes like this:

- Capital expenditures and capital budgets—that is, the use of investor capital—fall within corporate headquarters' domain. These items must be approved in light of corporate strategy. A division manager can make recommendations, but shouldn't feel it's his or her right to make these decisions.

- Division managers should seek advice from corporate headquarters in areas of legal significance affecting the entire company.

- Division managers should defer to corporate headquarters on those public relations issues affecting the image of the whole company—for example, in dealings with the news media. (Sales promotions on a particular product or service are divisional responsibilities, however.)

Division managers, for their part, should control operating expenses once the budget is approved. Pricing, manufacturing, marketing, engineering and sales should all fall within their purview, as should the development and implementation of new products once they are budgeted.

Conflict arises most frequently when the CEO approves your budget, then wants to get involved in approving ad campaigns or price discounts related to a promotion or in deciding whether or not to hire sales staff provided for in the budget.

In bridging such difficulties, keep the following points in mind:

- **An almost sacred desire to make the numbers is crucial.** It's going to really come down to a confidence factor. A CEO may back off because he doesn't want to mess up a winning game. But if the manager isn't making his numbers, the corporate types come out of the woodwork.

- **Maintain an ongoing dialogue with headquarters.** Corporate staff are often looking for the "gotchas." If they find something, they may go to the boss and say, "This guy has a problem and you don't know about it yet." It takes something away from them if you say beforehand, "I have a problem and need help with it."

  Remember that headquarters takes anything to do with the press or government very seriously—particularly in public companies. Trying to hold on to that is often fatal. Pass on anything relating to litigation of any substance, too.

- **Fostering divisional identity and esprit de corps should be a major objective.** One morale builder: Let your staff know that you are trying to get the best of them promoted to bigger positions in the company. This additional career ladder—nonexistent in a smaller firm—can be a powerful motivator. Once or twice a year, take the time to meet individually with your people on what the company is doing, from a total perspective, and where you see them making the biggest contribution.

- **New division managers should avoid the temptation to replace staff with their own people instantly.** You can often make your biggest mistakes early on, by not taking the time to see where people's strengths are so wait three to six months before making a switch, if you can.

- **Keep your own counsel.** Don't analyze the CEO's attitudes and failings for the benefit of subordinates. Don't weep on the CEO's shoulder regarding the shortcomings of division executives. If the CEO insists on a policy highly unpopular in your division, make your objections privately and, if that doesn't work, get behind it. Don't represent it as "headquarters' view" but as "our view." Public disagreement only announces to everyone that you are lacking in power to change the situation.

- **Demonstrate grace under pressure.** Like it or not, superiors do sometimes overrule division bosses while still holding them accountable for the division's profits and losses. There are times when you simply have to accept corporate intervention as though it were an act of God. In a conflict situation, present your case as ably as possible and, if overruled, resubmit it. If overruled again, drop it. This is a sign of true maturity on your part.

The Art of Dealing With Criticism

Praise is easy to take. Who doesn't want to be flattered? Criticism is another matter because it touches a sensitive nerve: our egos.

Unless it's given properly and under the right conditions, criticism is often perceived as an attack, says Robert Bies, assistant professor of organizational behavior at the Kellogg Graduate School of Management at Northwestern University, Evanston, IL. "A person's defenses go up when it comes to taking criticism," he says. "Nobody wants to hear what he or she thinks may be bad news."

As unpleasant as it is to give and take, criticism is essential for getting the best from your subordinates and from yourself.

Giving Criticism

- **Maintain a good climate.** It's a lot easier to give criticism if there is mutual respect, honesty and open communication between you and your subordinates, says Bies. Also, criticism is more likely to be well received—and acted upon—when given in a positive working environment.

- **Allow your people to correct their own mistakes.** When you discover that something is wrong, don't jump right in with criticism unless it's an emergency, suggests Bies. Allow your employees to work out their own problems. It might be a new project, work routine or procedure that takes getting used to. After you've waited an appropriate period of time (one to three days) and problems seem to persist, then step in and offer your criticism.

▪ ▪ **Technique:** Be concrete and specific. Avoid global criticism. Don't say: "You're doing a terrible job." Try: "The sales promotion literature on the new software needs tightening. It's a little long-winded and needs cutting. Let me show you what I'm talking about." Focus on the problem, not the person. When criticism is depersonalized and targeted, employees are less likely to feel singled out and put on the defensive. Specifics allow people to hear what you're saying and learn from it.

▪ **Allow your people to react.** Since criticism can be emotionally loaded, be prepared for a reaction. If you know the people you're criticizing well enough, you can anticipate their probable responses and be ready to deal objectively with them.

▪ **Pick an appropriate time.** Timing is crucial. Set aside a time that's good for both of you and that allows plenty of opportunity to talk without interruptions. Close your office door and tell your secretary to hold all your calls. If you prefer neutral ground, consider a conference room or a quiet corner of the company cafeteria.

Taking Criticism

Now the tables are turned. Taking criticism gracefully is a lot harder than giving it. But if you realize that criticism is essential for improvement—and advancement—it's easier to accept, stresses Bies.

The difficult part is objectively evaluating the criticism so you know whether it's warranted or not. "It's possible that your boss is misperceiving you," says Bies. "He or she may have made a mistake, or may not have all the information to understand the situation completely." To avoid misunderstandings, probe for details of your boss's complaint. Do not accept a statement like: "Your recent sales update was scattered and rambling." Counter with: "I'd appreciate it if you could show me where the report could be more concise." Weigh comments and objections carefully. As difficult as it is, put your ego aside so you see where you might have erred.

And if you have a boss who seldom offers criticism, Bies suggests

27

that you seek it out. "Some people are uncomfortable giving criticism and avoid the task. Ask plenty of questions so that it is easier for him or her to criticize your work."

▪▪ **Observation:** Whether you're giving it or taking it, criticism is essential for improving performance and the quality of work. You and your company both benefit from it when it is done properly.

Do You Promise More Than You Can Deliver?

In a dispute at the Metropolitan Opera, mezzo-soprano Maria Ewing cancelled her forthcoming appearances there. The singer claimed that the Met's artistic director, James Levine, was not planning to honor an oral commitment to conduct a revival and telecast of *Carmen* during the 1988–89 season, in which she was to have starred. Levine denied ever making such a promise.

Other opera stars were not surprised at the misunderstanding. Levine is known for his enthusiastic personal support of singers, which often seems to imply a go-ahead for projected roles and performances.

It's easy for any manager to be carried away during discussions with a favorite employee. You share an enthusiasm that enhances the relationship and makes for high productivity. But when you say, "We'll try out your project" or "I'd like to move you up before the end of the year," you may be instilling false hopes. And when the promotion never materializes, you'll be resented by the aggrieved employee and blamed, perhaps, by your boss if the person's dissatisfaction becomes known.

You can walk the fine line between commitment and caution if you keep the following guidelines in mind:

▪ Be aware that what you say and what the employee is hearing may actually be two different things.

▪ When you give an oral promise, qualify it: "Things may change at the last minute" or "I wouldn't count on it too much—for your own protection."

- Don't put anything in writing unless you are willing to be held to it.
- Be prepared to give up some popularity. It is better to disappoint employees—at first—than to mislead them.

▪ ▪ **Observation:** It's impossible to monitor yourself all the time. There will be unguarded moments when you want to make promises that seem perfectly reasonable at the time. But they may turn sour. Exercise a little restraint now and make good later, if that ever becomes a possibility.

Short-Fused Executives

— At the meeting last week, you blew up when colleagues couldn't see that your long-range plan was better than a co-worker's proposed alternative.

— Yesterday, the person filling in for your vacationing secretary collated documents incorrectly and was stuffing them in envelopes to be mailed when you caught the error and then exploded.

— When the president asked someone else to show him the details of an ad campaign for one of your division's products this morning, it was all you could do to keep yourself from telling him off.

Sound familiar? You may be the "short-fused" executive. You are likely to have a set of personality characteristics that can propel you to the very top—if you don't sabotage yourself first.

The "short-fuse" syndrome doesn't have an easy solution, psychologists emphasize. It's not like dressing for success. Still, there *are* both short- and long-term steps you can take to change.

Recognition, the first step, can be a hurdle. "It's like being an alcoholic," says Dr. Kenneth Blaker, a psychologist who teaches at Santa Clara University in California. "You struggle with denial, perhaps saying: 'I realize I've been a little volatile, but it hasn't interfered with my life.' Maybe later, people important to you become so alienated that you take action."

If you're a "short-fuser," you're also probably hard-driving and ambitious. You need to succeed not only in business, but on vacation as well.

You feel pressure from superiors, subordinates, family and peers. But the biggest pressure is likely to be internal. "Deep down, the person feels: 'I have to be better and better,' " explains Dr. Robert L. Reynes, a San Antonio, TX, therapist and clinical assistant professor of psychology at the Texas Health Science Center. "The issue of 'why' is never dealt with. Short-fused executives typically overreact when they feel they haven't measured up to their own standards."

You can increase your understanding and learn to anticipate trouble by keeping a log of each event that causes a blow-up. After a month or two, depending on the frequency of incidents, analyze them. What do the situations have in common? One element may be feeling a loss of control—something short-fusers dread more than most people.

If the trigger was a discussion of strategic planning, ask yourself these questions: Why do I have to be right all the time? What does it really mean if I compromise?

Many situations aren't upsetting only to short-fusers. "A boss encroaching on your turf encroaches on your self-esteem, and that troubles anyone," notes Dr. Reynes. "But while some executives will see the moment as one more illustration that we live in a world of people whose needs and wishes don't necessarily correspond to our own, the short-fuser experiences it as a permanent personal indictment. Deep down, the person may be feeling it's an ultimate confirmation of his or her own worthlessness."

Don't forget to check your log for basics. Are you becoming angry in situations where it might have been appropriate for you to give more detailed instructions at the beginning?

The next time you feel yourself about to blow up:

- Remind yourself that you haven't yet lost control.
- Remember that the old cliché about counting slowly to ten really works. It will give you a chance to think through whether or not your first reaction is the one you want to verbalize.
- Practice deep breathing. Dispelling rage into the atmosphere, rather than into your arteries, is likely to have positive physical and emotional effects. So will a long walk, a jog, or a game of squash.
- Talk to a trusted colleague. Go home and tell your spouse about the frustration you feel, not in a sense of shame, but in a sense of

irony. Life is not always fair and you can complain about bad breaks to a friend.

Finally, if a manager working for you is a short-fuser who disrupts the department, avoid putting the person on the defensive and making the problem worse. Dr. Blaker advises: "Don't start with: 'Productivity is down because you're responsible for hurting a lot of people's feelings.' Instead, try: 'We've got this problem. How do you think we can remedy it?' "

Dealing With Fear in the Workplace

In 1950, W. Edwards Deming was invited to Japan to help bring Japanese industry back to its feet. Although his management methods revolutionized Japanese quality and productivity, he did not gain full recognition in the United States until recently. One of the tenets of his philosophy is that workers who are prone to be fearful and anxious cannot perform effectively.

Many employees operate in a climate of fear. The result is stress, low productivity, medical and personal problems. In the absence of actual physical danger, what are employees afraid of?

Fear generally comes out of a feeling of powerlessness. Someone (the boss) or something (the organization) has control over crucial aspects of a person's life. Uncertain job security, performance appraisals, loss of status, failure to meet goals—all of these contribute to an employee's malaise.

Because there is a direct link between work climate and quality, a manager needs to provide a consistent, supportive environment. This means uncovering the sources of fear and taking steps to eliminate them:

— **Confusion.** Not knowing what the exact job requirements are can create anxiety. People are afraid to inquire too often about what is acceptable on the job and what is not, states Deming.

  Be sure that there is clear definition and an ongoing evaluation of what's needed. Then, supply the right training and tools.

— **Blame.** Employees are sometimes blamed for problems over which they have no control. For example, a report might be late

31

because approval is required from several departments, each with its own priorities. Always differentiate between a systems problem (e.g., computer failure) and a worker problem (lack of a specific skill).

— **Supervision: too much/too little.** A manager needs to be a coach without stifling employee initiative. When hiring new supervisors, screen your applicants carefully. You are looking for the ability to work as a team member and an openness to learning. Make it clear that management by intimidation is not acceptable, contrary to what some experts may maintain.

■ ■ **Observation:** "The fundamental problem in American business is that people are scared to discuss the problems of people," says Deming. When managers are committed to reducing fears, employees cooperate to ensure the long-term survival of the company and its effective operation.

Supervising a Friend

Some friendships formed in a business setting result in close personal bonds. But the situation can become complicated if one of you becomes the other's boss, especially if the subordinate's work slides. Often, you may be dealing with a conflict of feelings—your own ambivalence and your friend's. Here are some tips:

■ **Don't consider a "quickie" divorce.** Telling yourself that the friendship is over or that it really doesn't matter won't work. If it has been a genuine relationship up to this point, you won't believe this, and the problem won't go away that easily.

■ **Invoke the friendship on your side.** Perhaps your friend is using your friendship as a shield to hide something from you, or is protecting you from a problem because of the relationship. Whatever the case, you need to find out the truth. You might say something like: "Listen, you have no business avoiding discussing your problem with me. One very good reason is that I'm your boss and your friend. Now tell me what's going on."

- **Make it clear that you, too, are a "friend in need."** Any subordinate manager doing a poor job hurts you in two ways. First, your bosses are not pleased by the drop in your department's performance. Second, your support of the person as manager puts your judgment in question—particularly if the bosses are aware of your special relationship.

  Whatever the problem your friend describes—loss of confidence, alcohol or drug abuse, disgruntlement with the company, etc.,—point out that you can't afford to cover up for the person indefinitely.

- **Be firm.** Advise your friend to get some counseling, and make it clear that you'll do whatever you can to get the person back on track. But don't be afraid to administer a warning. "I also have to tell you that if we don't succeed, you may be out of a job." You will then be demonstrating that friendship is a two-way street.

Working With Your Hotshot Assistant

You know that you've got a brilliant assistant when he streamlines the company's distribution system in a way no one has ever thought of before—and it's only his first month on the job.

Or, your project team has just left a fact-finding meeting with a prospective client. In the taxicab on the way back, your new assistant spouts a plan that you all realize will become the winning proposal.

It's enough to make even the most self-confident manager feel a little uneasy. After all, no one wants to be shown up.

Dealing With the Talented Person Successfully

You don't have to be shown up. Instead, manage this "wunderkind" in a way that helps your career. "The key is to accept the notion that the brilliant assistant is either on the way up in the organization or on the way out," says Angelo Kinicki, an associate professor and specialist in organizational behavior at Arizona State University in Tempe. "If you help the person move up you'll have an ally in a parallel or superior position."

If his or her capabilities aren't fully used, the person will become bored and quit. Even worse, the person may stay and plot how to do end runs around you, causing political battles and turmoil.

Consider these suggestions:

- **Try to give the outstanding person highly visible assignments,** where the good job that's done will rebound to your credit and that of your assistant.

- **Propose the assistant for key interdepartmental or ad hoc committees if possible.** The exposure to top executives may prompt others to propose him or her for special projects, thus "inventing" a promotion for the star.

- **Avoid the temptation to call on the superstar for everything.** He or she only seems like Superman or Superwoman, and is as susceptible to burnout as anyone else.

Locking Horns With Organizational Values

Dealing with a brilliant assistant may require locking horns with your organization's cultural attitude toward creativity. "Many organizations are more concerned with appropriateness than with breakthroughs," says Larry Senn, chairman of the Senn-Delaney Group, a Long Beach, CA, consulting firm. "Appropriateness is an organizational value, and it could kill creativity."

Most creative people have a maverick streak. The more strictly defined appropriate behavior is, the less you'll find creative people in the firm. Occasionally, you may have to run interference for the talented associate who seems to march to a slightly different drummer.

Watch out for knee-jerk negativity, too. Almost no idea springs forth from its creator's lips in a perfectly developed state. It's all too easy—especially if you're feeling threatened—to pick out the negatives and dismiss an idea. Try to pick out the positives. Look for the opportunities inherent in an idea, and encourage your assistant to develop it.

Creative people can be particularly sensitive to authoritarian management styles. A more collegial approach, involving gently working toward general agreement, is sure to work better.

■ ■ Caution: Of course, it takes more than one brilliant assistant to make a department run well. In your enthusiasm over the hotshot, make sure that you don't ignore the rest of the staff. They may be having difficulties with envy and resentment of the superstar as it is. Give them some good assignments when you can, and don't miss an opportunity to say something positive like: "I notice you spent extra time on X project, and you did a really fine job on it." This will have an effect on their attitude toward the job in the future.

Are Others Stealing
the Credit You Deserve?

Consider the following examples of organizational credit-grabbing:

— Your boss has delegated the job of organizing the annual meeting to you, which his boss has assigned to him. You spend two weeks lining up speakers, reserving accommodations, organizing the agenda, writing and distributing invitations and drawing together a myriad of other details. At the closing banquet, your boss publicly accepts accolades for *his* fine job of organizing a successful meeting without mentioning *your* work even once.

— You've asked another manager to contribute to a proposal you're writing for submission to your mutual boss at a departmental meeting. The proposal is well received at the meeting, but you are annoyed when your colleague takes equal credit, referring often to "our research" and "when we were deciding on budget recommendations . . ."

— Over lunch with another manager, you ask her opinion of an idea you've devised for cutting costs. She seems lukewarm, so you're all the more taken aback when, two days later, she presents the idea to senior management as her own—and takes full credit for having conceived it.

Three examples, each illustrating this point: no matter how well you do the job, you cannot count on automatically getting the credit. Sometimes it's a honest oversight—the preoccupied boss who forgets to give public acknowledgement. Sometimes it's the result of a misunderstanding, or of others' overzealous efforts to shine, with no malice intended. Other times—well—whatever the case, you simply cannot trust that you will always get your just due. And, although you don't want to seem overbearing or nitpicky, you do want (and should have) the benefits you deserve. To this end, here are some practical suggestions:

- **Supply the pieces, but let others fit them together.** For instance, you can sometimes nail down credit by sharing it. An announcement at the departmental meeting to the effect, "I want to thank Jill for her assistance on this project," sets the record straight. So can a casual, "by the way" to the person who should know (your boss's boss) without stepping on toes. For example, "When I was researching Al's proposal, I found that the customers I talked to back up the library research on the competition."

- **Avoid accusations you can't prove.** You may be aware that your colleague has taken credit for your idea. But, making that public will not necessarily make others believe it. When you cast stones—even with full justification—people will always wonder who was right. And even when they have forgotten the specifics, they may still remember you as someone who made unproved accusations. It may be better to chalk it up to learning the hard way and put your energy into preventing a recurrence.

- **A discreet confrontation could help.** The credit-taker may or may not be aware of how you view the deed. If it was done without regard to your feelings, a quiet conversation could result in a public clarification. If the deed was done deliberately, then at least you've issued a warning.

- **Take preventive measures.** Once you've been burned, you'll probably resolve to take precautions in the future. Better to let others know about your efforts *while* you're doing the work rather than being informative after the fact. It need not sound immodest or aggressive—you are simply talking about the work you are doing. Or, if you have an idea, propose it publicly, with at least one witness. It may also help to put it in writing, but avoid such risky measures as a copy to your boss's boss of a proposal you've submitted to your own boss.

- **Consider whom you're dealing with.** When it's your boss who is not sharing credit, you need to exercise special diplomacy. Your approach will depend on your relationship and the circumstances, and it may be helpful to proceed with an attitude that assumes the boss intended no harm—that it was an oversight you simply want to correct. On the other hand, it may be more realistic to note that your boss assumes that taking credit for an employee's idea simply goes with the job.

- **Present a valid reason for seeking recognition.** This removes it from the personal realm and avoids overtones of blame or pushiness: "I think it would increase my credibility with our clients if they knew just how active I've been on their account." Or, a direct question, "Since I spent a good deal of time on this, do you think it would be appropriate to include my name under yours?"

■ ■ **Observation:** Lord Chesterfield advised his son that the world is divided between those who actually do the work and those who try to get the credit. Two hundred years later, people know their survival and success in an organization depends in part on making sure they get recognition for what they have accomplished. If they don't, then others will reach for it—just as they might for money left on the street—and their gain will then become your loss.

A Colleague Seeks Advancement
at Your Expense

John Ahearn has been burned twice now by someone he had long considered—well, not a close friend, perhaps, but a close colleague who, in the past, could usually be counted on for counsel and support when Ahearn needed them.

The latest incident occurred this morning. At the project meeting, Alan Thomas had taken the floor and systematically demolished the main points in John's proposal. A real hatchet job, although John had to admit that it came across as very polished and professional. And the executive vice president had bought it, leaving John alone, out on a rather shaky limb.

It's all of a piece, John thought. Alan is bucking for something—

I'm not sure what—and he's out to make himself look good. I just wonder how I should deal with the situation.

John Ahearn is in a not uncommon situation. It frequently happens that one of two people who have worked together on a friendly basis suddenly goes in a different direction. It may be due to personal ambitions, or a new organizational structure, or simply a change in attitude. But whatever the reason, the other person feels a sense of frustration and distrust.

If you find yourself in just such a situation, how can you best deal with it? Here are some prime considerations:

- **Assess your position.** There is always the possibility that, somehow, you may be viewing the situation from the wrong perspective or be out of step with current conditions in the organization. In John Ahearn's case, for example, his proposal may have had some major flaws—after all, top management did buy Alan Thomas's dissection of it.

  It might be wise, therefore, to take a new look at just where you are and just how you're doing. You may find that some pushing and prodding will be required to meet new demands, some changes in style will be necessary to deal with current conditions. Knowledge of this kind puts you in a stronger position to handle whatever lies ahead.

- **Maintain at least a surface cordiality.** There is really very little to be gained in cutting off every semblance of what was previously a friendly relationship. For one thing, it might be viewed as a lack of confidence in your own abilities. For another, it would close off an important line of communication. It's difficult to know what someone else is doing and thinking if the two of you are not speaking. So, at least outwardly, preserve the amenities—the "good morning," the pat on the back, the casual comments. At the same time, however . . .

- **Keep your own counsel.** At this juncture, it's probably wiser not to discuss your thinking, your plans or your work in any in-depth way with your colleague. You aren't sure what this person's motives are, you don't know the reasons for the change, so a certain amount of caution is definitely in order.

  What you really need, though, is some idea of what's going on, and you may be able to get this by asking discreet questions, doing more listening than talking, putting bits and pieces of conversations together. Just be wary of giving your own hand away.

- **Buttress your defenses.** Like John Ahearn, you may have been able to count on a close colleague for counsel and support in the past. But, at present, you cannot. That means that you are going to have to look elsewhere when you need assistance of one kind or another. This is the time, then, to look for new and stronger lines of support.

  It is also the time to put your best foot forward—in the work that you do, in the ideas that you contribute, in the plans that you propose, in the dealings that you have with people up the line. The better you look, the less you have to be concerned about the possible harm in a change in relationships.

- **■ Observation:** Personal relationships—good or bad—are an intrinsic part of any organization. But they can seldom be taken for granted. This is why, when a long-time relationship begins to change, you have to be alert to prevent yourself from viewing the change as necessarily working to your disadvantage. You'll find the change might be for the better.

When You're on the Road to CEO

Some children dream of becoming doctors and astronauts, and some adults dream of becoming CEO. Haven't you often felt that you could do just as good a job—if not a better one—than some of the CEOs you've met?

Perhaps you do have the makings of a leader: People look up to you—and not just your subordinates. You're a resource, a diplomat without portfolio, a consultant without the title. At meetings, you cut through irrelevancies to the heart of a problem. If you can't solve it, you know what steps are necessary in finding a solution. You may, indeed, be destined for bigger things.

There are no guarantees that you'll make it, but you stand a better chance if you can help matters along. Some pointers:

39

- **Pick the right spot.** In certain industries, individuals are advancing rapidly. Other areas are sluggish and will probably remain so. Follow the business news closely and consider shifting to an industry that is enjoying a growth spurt. Or, if you've got foresight and guts and you're willing to go out on a limb, try a company that is in the throes of turning itself around.

- **Maintain relationships.** As the prize gets bigger, the game gets rougher. You'll need to hold on to a solid core of supporters through good times and bad.

- **Know when to let go.** You also need to know when to let relationships fade. It may be coldblooded, but if you are single-minded about your goal, you can't afford to hang on to people on their way out. There is a risk of being tainted by association.

- **Invite feedback on your style.** There's often a discrepancy between how you see yourself and how others see you. You must be perceived as having leadership qualities. If you are not receptive to criticism, you'll never find out what other people think.

- **Welcome risk.** It's a chance to be innovative, according to Walter Wriston, former CEO of Citicorp. You'll probably fail from time to time, but you risk even more by being too cautious.

- **Stay current.** Keep up with changes in your field. Take refresher courses, attend trade meetings, read the literature. If you are considered out of step, you will suffer setbacks in your quest.

- **Develop inner resources.** The higher you go, the more isolated you will become. The toll can be great: Family life and personal time fall by the wayside. If you're dogged in your determination, you must learn to make the necessary tradeoffs and live with them.

- **Go with your intuition** even though it might lead you into terra incognita. Take a cue from Armand Hammer, who says, "Whenever I see everyone rushing in one direction, I know it's time to move the other way."

- **Make a career plan,** but don't be restricted by it. If you see that your career has taken another turn, allow yourself the flexibility to change. A timetable needs constant reevaluation. Even if you don't make it to CEO, you'll still have the satisfaction of doing your best.

Taking a Step up on the Ladder

You've been hankering for that promotion for a long time. When it finally happens, you're surprised to find that you are in a strange new world. Not only is your job difficult, but your relationships have changed. To your former peers, you're no longer one of the gang.

Personal relationships seem more stilted, even strained. Can you be both boss and friend? What can you say—what can you do—to ease the transition for yourself and for those you now manage?

If the situation is awkward, here's what you can do:

- **Confront resistance.** If you sense jealousy, hard feelings or general tension on the part of some employees, meet with them individually to find out what's bothering them. Let them know that you realize it's a difficult transition for all concerned. But make it clear that you need and are counting on their cooperation.

- **Be yourself.** Don't let your promotion go to your head. Few things turn employees off faster than the manager who lords it over others. Your promotion is recognition of your attributes and contributions. If you prided yourself on being accessible and accommodating before, continue to be that way.

- **Say "no" tactfully.** There will be times when you will have to turn down a former peer's suggestion or request. How do you do it without giving a "power-hungry" aura? Here are some tactful responses that fit the situation:

   —"It's contrary to company policy; my hands are tied."

   —"Your approach is too costly. I need a suggestion that will meet our budget."

   — Offer an alternative, or show the person an approach he or she can take.

- **Remember what you wanted yesterday.** It was not so long ago that you wanted to be told the reasons behind your assignment, thirsted for words of encouragement and praise, and looked for consistent supervision. Remember what you wanted in a manager

41

yesterday and you will have a reliable guide to what your people expect from you today.

■ ■ **Observation:** A promotion is not a coronation. You were promoted to do a job and have done your previous job well. Therefore, the sooner you settle into the new routine, the sooner your staff will, too. Respect will be gained, without the loss of friendship.

Making the Mentor Connection

Mentoring isn't new. What is new is that it's more important as a career tool for senior managers than it was in the past.

The old theory about mentoring was that it was a stage you went through and eventually outgrew as your career advanced. This is no longer true. At the higher rungs of the corporate ladder, career paths are more complicated, pointing up the benefits of either having a mentor or acting as one.

Realizing the importance of mentoring, a number of prominent companies (Johnson & Johnson, Merrill Lynch, Bell Labs, National Cash Register) have established formal mentoring programs. Bright managerial prospects are assigned a mentor rather than having them go through the accidental, often serendipitous, process of finding one on their own.

Why Mentoring Is so Important Now

- In an uncertain corporate environment, it is an excellent way to encourage and tap creativity. The mentor can create a safe harbor so that a protégé can develop new ideas. It also encourages idea-bouncing, which often leads to innovation.

- Mentors can also bend the organization's rules so that protégés can test their wings and realize their potential at the same time.

- It is beneficial in cross-cultural corporations. *Example:* the growing number of Japanese companies operating in the U.S. The mentor acts as a bridge between these two cultures, facilitating the learning of customs, rules and protocol, benefitting both the mentor and protégé.

- Political leverage. Working with other managers, the protégé can provide the mentor with valuable information from above and below. Similarly, the mentor can open up important political doors for the protégé.

Get Yourself Picked

How do you find a mentor if your company doesn't have a program? The operative word is visibility, which can be accomplished by:

1. **Getting assigned to projects** where you can contribute your talents.
2. **Writing reports.** If there are none in the offing, volunteer for some when the opportunity arises. When they're completed, hand deliver them. Constant interaction is vital for establishing a comfortable rapport with a potential mentor.
3. **Asking questions.** It's an excellent way to make yourself known and air your ideas and opinions.

There are many drawbacks to mentoring. The mentor you find may not be the best teacher for you or your mentor may fall out of favor with senior management, taking you out, too. Here are some suggestions for avoiding these traps:

- When looking for a mentor, know what you want from the relationship. Then hold prospective mentors up to certain criteria. What do they hope to gain from the relationship in terms of work and political goals? How strong are their alliances?
- Are these people good teachers and motivators? Some mentors will oversee your career but do little to enhance your knowledge of the job. At some point, you'll have to stand by yourself.
- Might you pose a threat to your mentor? Some people are very good when they're mentoring several levels down the organization, but when a protégé begins to draw even, new rules come into play. Try to find out how your mentor treated other protégés who have worked closely with him or her.

- Never burn bridges between you and the organization. Don't assume that you're protected by the mentor or part of that person's group. You're still a low person on the organizational chart. No matter how good your relationship with your mentor, be wary of a false sense of security.

- In the course of the relationship with your mentor, ask if your goals are really being met. If not, why not?

- Maintain your alliances. Avoid factions and establish good relationships with everyone. Avoid political hassles.

- If your situation is not improving after the first year in a mentor relationship, consider finding a new mentor. This can be accomplished diplomatically by gradually easing into a new relationship, thus painlessly loosening your tie with your former mentor. This is far wiser than making a hasty break of some kind.

Just How Effective Is Your Network?

The climate of some organizations is more conducive to informal cooperation than that of others. But, whatever the tone of relationships where you work, your job will go more smoothly if you build a trusting rapport with your colleagues and other employees. Here are some ways you can benefit from widening your personal network:

- **Exchange of information.** What's the top brass thinking? How is a multidepartmental project really going? What personnel changes are in the wind, and what implications does that have for your group? Who has been talking to whom? Answers to questions like these are often gotten faster through casual conversation than through official channels.

- **Quick answers.** How reliable is a given supplier? What's that client's account number? Whom should you call at headquarters?

Is there a trade association that might supply you with background facts for your speech? Who is temporarily taking over a sick colleague's work? If you have the right in-house contacts, you get immediate answers with one phone call.

- **Support.** You want to change a procedure. You have an idea you'd like to try out. You disagree with a proposal your boss is considering. The larger your network, the better your chances of getting the support and cooperation you need.

- **Emergency assistance.** You have two people out sick, and a big job just appeared; you need to "borrow" someone from another work group. Or, you've got an irate client on the phone; you need to find an answer while you put her on "hold." Or, your department runs short of supplies in the middle of a rush job; you can't wait for the requisition process. Well-placed friends can help you out when you're in need.

You have to work at building a wider network. Here's how:

- **Get connected** through friends you already have. Being a friend-of-a-friend is probably the quickest way to develop mutual trust and cooperation.

- **Stop to talk** when you see people you would like to know better. You might even go out of your way to improve your chances of running into them.

- **Make the first move** by broaching common problems and asking friendly questions. The best first move is to offer assistance of some kind.

- **Share credit.** When something goes well that involves your work group and someone else's, express your appreciation to the other person for your mutual success. When others congratulate you, be sure to mention your colleague's contribution.

- ■ **Observation:** The key to effective networking is establishing trust. You can blow a whole chain of relationships with one small indiscretion. If you have a reputation for discretion, your network will continue to grow, and this is certain to strengthen your position in the long run.

Always Stay on Top of Your Promotion

A promotion is a victory, an accomplishment to be proud of. As excited and enthusiastic as you are to make your mark in the new job, there are unseen stumbling blocks on that higher rung that can trip you up if you're not very careful.

Here are some common problems that recently promoted managers encounter and suggestions for handling them:

— **Letting go.** This is one of the biggest difficulties for newly promoted managers. They are more familiar with the problems of the old job and know how to fix them. And they usually feel more comfortable operating in the realm where they excelled.

Suggestion: Withdraw by delegating to people you have confidence in. The more you feel your staff is up to the job, the easier it will be. Reassess each person's skills from your new perspective.

It takes self-discipline to break the umbilical cord. When you are tempted to step in and take over, remind yourself that this can backfire. It diverts energy from your new work at a time when staying focused is crucial to success.

— **Handling resentment and jealousy.** Someone who competed for the promotion may now report to you. Angry and hurt, he or she may spread rumors, refuse to cooperate, and rally others to do the same.

Suggestion: Try ignoring the sabotage for a time; it may play itself out. If it doesn't, confront the person. Cite specific things that were done or said—the letter to a customer that incorrectly implied you were to blame for a missed deadline, the remark you overheard about how you got the job through unethical ploys. Show how it will be to the person's benefit to support you. Point out how productivity is dependent on cooperation and harmony, and that the lack of it reflects on everyone involved. If the problem persists, warn the troublemaker that efforts to undermine your authority or stifle productivity will seriously damage the individual's future.

— **Getting a handle on new job requirements.** "Each step brings more freedom," notes Dr. Jim Lister, an industrial psychologist with Byron Harless, Reid & Associates, Inc., in Jacksonville, FL. "The initial response to that is often anxiety."

Some people tend to approach the new job in the same way as the old, out of habit and a natural desire to continue methods that proved effective.

People new to management may face their first experience directing a team—a different task from supervising a secretary. A move from first to second line management requires other kinds of skills.

Suggestion: To help yourself switch gears, get a precise job description from both your boss and your predecessor, if possible. Get a firm grasp on your old and new responsibilities and what they call for. Then compare and contrast.

If this is your first management position, consider taking a management training seminar or a suitable course or two at a nearby university or college.

When moving to second line management, expect to be less involved in the day-to-day and more involved in long-range strategic planning. Says Lister, "Your success will depend more on judgment skills, the teamwork of your employees, and your ability to coach and advise rather than supervise."

— **Adjusting to a new boss relationship.** You may report to a different person with a new set of needs and expectations. Or—often more difficult—you may keep the same boss, but the dynamics of the relationship will change. Be aware that your skill at reading and responding to your boss can either smooth or aggravate the transition into your new role.

Suggestion: "Strike a balance," says Lister. "Be independent and bring something new to the position, but stay within the parameters of what the boss wants and respects." One boss might take well to formal, written status reports; another may go for casual chats to learn what's been happening.

"Keep assessing how your boss responds," adds Lister. "You don't want to be a sycophant, but stay attuned so you can judge when a different approach might be wise."

■ ■ **Observation:** Lister points out that people often think a higher position means working longer and harder. They overlook the more important difference—a necessary change in their attitude.

Making the Grade in a New Position

More and more managers are on the move. By the time they reach their late forties, general managers have assumed from three to nine managerial posts. All else being equal, a manager's functional background, experience and special competencies will determine how that person takes charge, according to Dr. John J. Gabarro, professor of organizational behavior at the Harvard Business School, who carefully monitored the management experiences of 14 new executives over a three-year period.

Some managers make the transition in easy, sure strides; others falter and fail. Here are some touchstones for a safe voyage:

- **Know your strengths and limitations.** If you are moving into a new position within your company, one where your experience is clearly applicable, you are most likely to succeed. But if you are an outsider, or your experience is not directly related to the new post, then your taking charge is going to be much more difficult.

    Gabarro challenges the myth of the jack-of-all trades superman-ager who can jump into any troubled area and straighten it out overnight. New managers are not doomed, but they must recognize their knowledge gaps and compensate for them by doing extra research and by drawing on support and expertise from others.

- **Know exactly what your new bosses expect of you.** "Front-end work is essential," cautions Gabarro. Anyone who takes on new responsibilities without a thorough understanding of what must be done is gliding on very thin ice. In every successful transition Gabarro examined, new managers made their mandates explicit: no gray areas, no assumptions, no mysteries.

    Successful new managers never lose sight of their need for management support. Some differences with bosses are predictable, usually in matters of control and delegation, but new managers are advised to take the initiative in ironing away the wrinkles. They also need to be careful about keeping their superiors informed, especially of changes, in the early stages of their tenure.

- **Monitor your working relationships.** Three of the four managers who failed in Gabarro's study had poor rapport with key subordinates; all were unable to communicate effectively with their bosses. Rivalry, disagreement about performance goals, conflicts in managerial style—many things can break down the relationship. A common explanation is that new managers fail to spell out their expectations to subordinates. Let your people know what you have in mind.

  General Electric tries to ease the taking-charge process by running assimilation meetings where new managers and their key subordinates talk about expectations and problems early on.

- **Be patient.** You are going to be walking the newcomer's tightrope for longer than you probably anticipated. Gabarro's executives moved through five carefully defined stages—taking hold, immersion, reshaping, consolidation and refinement. Each lasted up to six months, so the proof of their tenure took two years or more. Most of the new managers did not make any significant personnel, marketing or organizational moves until they had been in their jobs for a year. They spent their apprenticeships learning about the product, the people and the problems while making an effort to keep the business running at the same time.

- **Observation:** Not unexpectedly, Gabarro highlights the importance of experience ("When a New Manager Takes Charge," *Harvard Business Review*, May-June 1985). He acknowledges, however, that managers without optimal experience will always be moved into new jobs. The taking-charge process may be more difficult for them, but this very experience is essential to advancement into the upper levels of management.

Opportunity for the Acting Manager

If you have followed Laurence A. Tisch's career at CBS, you've seen a good demonstration of how serving as an acting or interim manager can result in an official promotion. After five months as the acting CEO, Tisch was formally appointed as both CEO and president.

As you're probably aware, this was really quite an exceptional situation. Tisch's performance clearly satisfied the directors; both positions were open; and Tisch also happened to be co-CEO and chairman of the board (and a major shareholder) of the Loews Corporation, a major CBS stockholder.

In contrast, the circumstances under which you might be asked to serve as an acting manager may not be quite as favorable. They seldom are.

You may be temporarily filling a senior position that's usually staffed by someone whose background—in domestic and international R&D, for example—is considerably broader than your own, which might be limited to engineering. On the other hand, you might be replacing your boss, who may or may not be returning to the position in question from a special assignment or an extended disability leave.

Still, even if you don't win an outright promotion, serving as acting manager could give you the experience you need to get promoted to a different position down the road. To make the most of your opportunity, consider the following:

- **Time period.** "Go into the situation realistically and find out what the expectations are," advises Dr. Samuel Rabinowitz, associate professor of management and organizational behavior at the Rutgers University School of Business in Camden, NJ.

  If you're filling in for a relatively short time, your authority will be more limited than if you're stepping into an open position. If you are pinch-hitting, you should be able to talk to the person you're replacing before he or she goes away, says Rabinowitz.

  You'll want to learn the individual's system and try not to contradict procedures that were set up over a long time period. If the person used approach A and you try approach B, you'll confuse everyone. "The manager coming back could interpret it as a real slap in the face," says Rabinowitz.

- **Relationships.** It's important to clearly establish the scope of your authority with your new boss, as well as with your new subordinates. This will help prevent territorial clashes, not only with these individuals, but also with your new colleagues in senior management. If you will be serving as the acting manager for an open position, this is even more crucial. Your mandate is apt to be less clear-cut since it's not known when—and if—someone will be taking over from you.

50

- **Prospects.** Try to find out what has happened to other interim managers at your firm, suggests Rabinowitz. Were they promoted more quickly, relieved of their duties or any variation in between? This information can help strengthen your case, should you decide to press for the official promotion and the raise that goes with it.

  Even though you may feel now that advantage is being taken of you, it's important to prove that you can successfully handle the additional responsibilities a promotion would be sure to bring.

- ■ **Observation:** However long your stint as interim manager lasts, bear in mind that you could end up in your previous position. To avoid sabotaging your future, don't let your temporary assignment alienate you from your former peers. You're bound to need their continuing support, no matter what happens to you in the future.

How High Is High Enough for You?

A study of 100 plateaued managers and 100 upwardly mobile managers revealed a surprising similarity: The two groups did not differ significantly in terms of satisfaction with their professional and personal lives. Most rated their satisfaction at four or five on a five-point scale.

"These findings run counter to stereotypical attitudes toward career plateaus," says Janet Near, professor of management at Indiana University (Bloomington), who conducted the study. "There has traditionally been a stigma attached to staying put." Since there are more strivers than top positions, it's inevitable that most careers will level out somewhere short of the executive suite. Interestingly, the majority of executives are standing still, often due to factors unrelated to performance: a boss who won't budge; a recent acquisition or merger that creates duplicate jobs; or even "voluntary plateauing."

How do you determine your personal comfort level? And, once you have found it, how can you make peace with it and ensure against boredom and burnout?

- **Define what success means to you.** Unfortunately, most people don't do this until forced by a layoff or other crisis, human resource experts say. Often, they discover that until that happened they were motivated by criteria set by others: employer, mentor, parents, spouse or community.

Do some serious soul-searching, suggests Near. Try to separate your fantasies from reality so you can get a firm grip on what's actually possible. Whatever your definition of success, you may discover that you can stop your climb and still feel that you've really achieved it.

- **Examine your priorities.** To reach that number one spot, it's necessary to make 80 to 90 percent of your life job-related, say the experts. A growing number of executives are not willing to make the sacrifice. Many people are rejecting the 'bigger is better' philosophy and focusing on a higher quality of life instead. For some, this means finding areas outside of work from which to gain satisfaction and enjoyment—family, hobbies, community activities, alternate careers.

- **Enhance your job.** Although many of the satisfied plateaued managers Near studied held the same title for up to 20 years, few continued doing the same work for the entire time. The reason: A middle management job can always be made more interesting. The key is to take more control over your work. Some ways you can add to your responsibilities are by taking on special projects, or joining another team in a pursuit that catches your interest (such as teaching an in-house training course). You can also set your own goals in addition to those your boss sets for you.

- ▪ **Observation:** If your organization has an "up or out" policy, consider making a lateral move to another organization. In companies with a narrow career track to the top, 60 to 70 percent of executives will not "make it" in the eyes of top management. Even those who feel content to stand still may find the pressure and stigma uncomfortable. A more appropriate place may be with an employer that provides more avenues for achievement.

The Importance of Being Earnest
About Politics

Ever wonder why an executive who makes a million-dollar mistake can get off with a reprimand, while another who does an expert job is let go? Maybe performance is not the determining factor when cutbacks have to be made. This is what a number of executives are discovering, and it's a bewildering lesson.

"Part of our job is to find out how a person ended up in our offices," says Dr. Adela Oliver, president of Oliver Human Resource Consultants, Inc., a New York-based executive out-placement and organization development firm. "It's very difficult for some people to understand that even if their performance is exemplary, they are sometimes more vulnerable than individuals who aren't quite as good at what they do— but who understand the unspoken rules of the game."

Even if the reason given for the termination relates to performance, the underlying cause is often a lack of political savvy. Doing a job well is certainly important, says Oliver, but it is not enough. A political lapse or blunder can make the difference when choices have to be made by top management. And if you choose to remove yourself from the political arena, you could end up in no man's land.

Some managers fail to recognize a recurring pattern in themselves: They do their jobs well; then, when the crunch comes, they are out because they are politically naive. Oliver describes some common traps:

— **"Failure to salute the general."** Regardless of what you think of your boss, you must make him or her look good. Even if the boss is on temporary assignment—many companies rotate executives—and even if you've been in the firm much longer, you must show respect for the position.

　　Your boss may appear to take no notice of slights. However, you can be sure the information is being stored. "Comes the day of judgment," warns Oliver, "and the boss will have you eliminated."

— **Burning your bridges.** No one moves up the ladder alone, but some people tend to forget those who helped them. They don't give credit where it's due—and worse, some ruthlessly try to crush those who supported them along the way.

When the crisis comes and there are no allies who will stand up for you, you are an easy target for a layoff.

— **The office romance**—always risky, however discreet you think you are. It's seldom enough of a reason per se to get you fired unless it has affected the productivity of your department. But when your boss is asked to cut staff, you may be the first on the hit list.

— **Bypassing the boss.** "In the long run, it will always be lethal," states Oliver. Suppose your boss's boss singles you out for a particular assignment and asks you not to tell your own boss. Very flattering, of course. But beware. The special circumstances will undoubtedly come to light, and you'll be surprised to find that your "patron" is staunchly on your boss's side.

▪ ▪ **Observation:** Outplacement candidates often need to be politically trained, says Oliver, who recommends certain eye-opening books to her clients.*

"When cutbacks occur, it's like musical chairs," she further explains. "When the music stops, there may not be a chair for you if you aren't politically agile. Then you're out of the game."

---

*These include: *Art of War,* by Sun Tzu, written in 500 B.C. (Delacorte, $7.95); *Book of the Five Rings,* by Musashi, written in the mid-17th century (Overlook Press, $9.95); *Games Mother Never Taught You: Corporate Gamesmanship for Women,* by Betty Lehan Harragan (Warner $5.95); *The Prince,* by Machiavelli, written in 1513 (available from several publishers).

When You're Picking a Successor

You're enhancing your chances of being promoted if you have a strong successor in the wings, stresses Michael G. Zey, author of *The Right Move* (available in some libraries). As soon as you're comfortable in your job, start looking for candidates who can replace you.

There are three important reasons why you ought to be grooming a successor, according to Zey:

1. **If you hope to move up, it's vital to have someone to replace you.** "Just because you're doing an excellent job and you're well liked, don't assume you'll be promoted," says Zey. It may not happen or it could take a very long time. Many organizations will not promote you until they have an acceptable person to replace you.

   Cover your bases by not letting your company go through the process of replacing you. Replace yourself. You're strengthening your career, and at the same time sparing your boss the time and aggravation it takes to find and train your successor.

2. **It makes you look good.** The glory is shared by both you and your successor. When this person receives accolades after taking over your job, it has a halo effect. "You're viewed as more valuable and competent because you chose well and trained well," Zey further explains.

3. **You gain an ally.** Since you will have had a history together, your successor can be valuable to you in his or her new job. "If there is a crisis (layoffs, budget cuts, departmental restructuring), you can depend upon this person to provide you with grapevine information you may not have," says Zey.

When You're Choosing a Replacement

Along with the essential qualities necessary for the job, "look for someone you can trust and who shares the same goals as you do," says Michael Zey. "Don't just pick a bright performer. Instead, find someone whom you can relate to and identify with." It is also crucial for your successor to have organizational savvy. "He or she must know how to play the game well," Zey stresses.

Train this person as you would any new hire, with a few important exceptions. "You have to be willing to give your potential successor extra time," Zey says. Along with imparting managerial skills, you have to let him or her observe and watch you work. "Many executives are reluctant to do this," he adds. "They prefer to operate in secrecy. Even though it may seem inconvenient, you must bring this person into your private fold." This is role participation, far different and much more effective than role modeling.

Instead of encouraging emulation, you must involve your candidate in the managerial process. Let him or her make decisions. If there is a problem to be solved, ask for ideas on how to do it. Let this person work with you on important projects like the budget, for example. Or if taking phone calls from irate customers is part of your job, let your successor listen in on conversations to hear the interaction. If the opportunity arises, take your candidate on business trips to observe how you work with sales and marketing people, as well as customers.

In sum, try to work your potential successor into your daily schedule so that he or she has the opportunity to see the whole job and to ask plenty of questions. Zey estimates that it could take anywhere from six months to a year to train a successor, depending upon the nature of the job and the amount of time you can afford to devote to the task.

▪ ▪ **Observation:** The training process ought to be done openly. "People around you should be aware of what's going on," says Zey. "After all, organizations are hierarchies and this is the way things get done. Initially, there may be hurt feelings, but there is nothing you can do about it. People will quickly accept the situation as a fact of corporate life."

A Lateral Move Can Lead Upward

As with many successful managers, your first few promotions probably came fairly quickly. Yet now that you're starting to feel limited in your present position, you may find that the direct path to senior management is blocked by skilled superiors, who don't look as though they're going to change jobs in the near future.

Or perhaps your organization is trying to flatten itself out and eliminate layers.

"Not pursuing lateral moves in these kinds of situations is the single biggest mistake managers make in their career paths over a number of years," advises James Walker, president of J.F. Walker Co., a consulting firm in Louisville, Kentucky.

Whether you remain with your present company or shift to a new one, you'll need to assess the following variables:

- How large and/or stratified the organization is. Too many layers can limit movement between divisions or departments.

- How fast it's growing—and by what means. More opportunities are created through internal development than through various acquisitions.

- What percentage of all promotions are filled internally. Some companies select their top managers from outside.

What Kind of Move?

You may decide that you need experience in a field that's closely aligned to your current one. For instance, an R&D manager might do well to transfer to operations. A product manager might gain by shifting from marketing to sales. The combination of the two could actually give you a better chance at senior management than trying to take the fast track.

Also consider moving farther afield if you have reason to believe that you'd be successful. Transferring laterally from managing an R&D function to managing a marketing operation, for example, would be very valuable experience for the individual, and good for the organization.

Too radical a move, like switching from finance to advertising, could be questionable, however, because the farther you move from your area of expertise, the longer it takes for you to become effective in your new position.

Evaluate what kind of management experience you lack for the career path you've chosen, and where you can obtain it. For example, if you've always worked in a growth area, you could gain by managing one that's declining as well, if doing that ever becomes a possibility.

> ▪ ▪ **Observation:** Naturally, you'll want to avoid any shift to a position with less impact and less authority than you currently have. But any move that increases the number of people and dollars you're responsible for is almost always considered a step up, even though your title may remain the same.

Taking a Temporary Step Down

"Joe will be leaving us soon and we want you to fill his role for a while. You will, of course, maintain your present responsibilities as well."

Directives like this are becoming increasingly common, as organizations embark on acquisitions, mergers and downsizing to meet competition. Salaries are often the first costs to be cut, and middle managers are asked to double up on responsibilities, assuming the dual roles of first- and second-line manager.

What are some of the prime difficulties of maintaining these two responsibilities simultaneously? Among them are:

— **Balancing conflicting roles.** A first-line manager is typically dealing with a homogenous, single function, and directing its day-to-day operations. In contrast, a second-line manager carries more heterogeneous responsibilities covering a larger scope, and must integrate diverse functions and resolve conflicting priorities.

   The two jobs require different skills and outlooks. To switch hats several times in a given day, therefore, can be extremely time-consuming and energy-draining, and sometimes confusing.

The first-line job requires so much attention to detail that it is easy to get mired in minutiae, and difficult to extricate yourself, notes a manager who's had to fill both roles. "When you must suddenly switch to your second-line role, it can be hard to see the forest for the trees."

This is especially true for a manager who has not held a first-line position in several years, or who has skipped over that particular position altogether.

— **Compensating for staffing deficits.** When a first-line manager is terminated, other positions are usually eliminated as well. This can seriously overload the system's capacity. Remaining workers must handle more tasks. Consequently, stress mounts, efficiency suffers, and morale plummets. The manager is then faced with lower productivity and larger employee relations problems—a potentially lethal combination.

— **Information loading.** When you hold two jobs simultaneously, more pieces of paper cross your desk. As the piles build, it's easy to get frantic and feel guilty for letting things slide. Tension inevitably mounts and affects every area of the manager's job.

— **Adjusting self-image.** Second-line managers see themselves as people who orchestrate and/or supervise the overall picture, but delegate the everyday details to lower-level people. Managers who feel uncomfortable about filling a role that they think is beneath them tend to communicate the following message to employees: "Don't get the wrong idea. This is not really me. My job is much more important."

This sort of attitude lowers the value of the first-line position in employees' minds, as well as their respect for it. Eventually, it can also lead them to perceive the manager as arrogant, self-involved and uncaring, and undermine their respect for him or her.

In addition, managers face the ego blow of being "demoted." The step down may even threaten their personal identity. This can generate a good deal of resentment and stress. The stress tends to be contagious to employees, and to have a counterproductive effect on the entire operation.

Suggestions

- **Start by analyzing the overall system.** The Hay (consulting) Group has found that it is possible to downsize by 20% with little difficulty when managers begin with good planning. "As soon as you are informed of the downsizing, take a few days to study the management systems in each area to determine where you can increase efficiency," its consultants advise. Right at the start, look for ways to simplify procedures and cut waste. This will solve several problems: It will reduce information loading and thereby cut drains on your time and energy; diminish the stress of role loading for employees and thereby ease employee relations; and allow the opportunity to plan ways to avoid favoritism.

- **Don't fight the system.** Managers create problems for themselves by resisting the order to assume dual roles. Those who make peace with the situation are better able to adjust their self-image. It helps to accept the situation as temporary and to approach it with a sense of humor. And don't forget: The manager who resists will then be remembered as a detractor, while the one who accepts gracefully soon earns a name as a willing contributor.

- **Do not overexplain to employees.** Do your job well and avoid explaining the obvious. Employees understand what is going on and will follow your lead if you make the transition gracefully.

- ■ **Observation:** Your temporary step down can actually be a valuable learning experience. When you return to your single role as second-line manager, you will probably take along increased understanding and empathy for your first-line position from a new perspective, and become aware of adjustments that could help you perform better. This will prove to be worthwhile when you move ahead at a later date.

Practical Intelligence
for On-the-Job Success

New psychological research is sharply focusing on people's practical intelligence: The special talents with which we meet life's daily challenges.

Two Minds at Work

A sampling of the research can be found in *Practical Intelligence* (Cambridge University Press, 110 Midland Ave., Port Chester, NY 10523; $21.95), edited by Robert J. Sternberg of Yale University and Richard K. Wagner of Florida State University. Most of the investigators believe there are two intelligences at work in people: a practical, experiential intelligence that makes our daily decisions and has nothing to do with IQ, and a rational intelligence that unravels the mysteries of math and literature, offering some logical explanations for our actions.

Sternberg and Wagner have studied the influence of what they call "tacit knowledge" on the practical intelligence of successful business executives. "This tacit knowledge, which is rarely verbalized," they say, "enables workers to meet the often unwritten and unspoken demands of their jobs."

Although the specific contents of tacit knowledge may differ from job to job, the basic framework remains.

For example, "the ability to sell is a kind of persuasion everybody needs," notes Sternberg. "You sell yourself when you meet someone; you sell your ideas or point of view; you sell when you negotiate a deal. Sales is a skill that demands a specific kind of practical intelligence."

Using a New Test

Wagner and Sternberg built a test around a dozen work-related situations with a choice of responses based on interviews with successful executives. The test measures three types of practical intelligence: self management (e.g., an ability to motivate yourself); managing others (how to reward); and managing your own career (how to enhance your reputation).

Here is a typical question—one that measures the thinking needed to advance one's career:

— **Your year on the job has been generally favorable.** Performance ratings for your department are at least as good as they were before you became manager, and perhaps even better.

You have two assistants. One is quite capable. The other just seems to go through the motions but is of little real help. You believe that although you are well-liked, there is little that would distinguish you in the eyes of your superiors from nine other managers at a comparable level. Your goal is rapid promotion to the top.

The following is a list of things you are considering. Rate the importance of each:

__a. Find a way to get rid of the "deadwood"—i.e., the less helpful assistant.

__b. Participate in a series of panel discussions on local public TV.

__c. Make sure your superiors are made aware of your important accomplishments.

__d. Accept a friend's invitation to join an exclusive country club to which many higher-level executives belong.

__e. When making decisions, give a great deal of weight to the way your superiors like things done.

The most successful executives—54 managers, 19 of whom were from the top 20 Fortune 500 companies—tended to rank their responses in the same order: e, a, c, b, d.

Those who scored highest were found to have more management experience and higher salaries than those who did less well.

Implications for Managers

The research on practical intelligence offers fresh insights into the special competencies of successful managers. For example, two Boston psychologists, David McClelland and George O. Klemp Jr., compared outstanding performers with mediocre ones. The most effective do the following:

- Push hard for concrete details when confronted with ambiguity.
- Gather problem-solving data from as wide a range of sources as possible.
- Find unusual analogies to explain their insights.
- Consistently anticipate the impact of their decisions on others, and never hesitate to confront people.

- ▪ **Observation:** While our IQs may be fixed, some psychologists believe that practical intelligence can be enhanced: We can be trained to work smarter. This is good news indeed for those who want to scale the executive ladder.

THE POLITICS OF TEAMWORK

Your Department May Be Losing Its Memory

Managers today must be forward-looking, but there's a danger that a work group's past can gradually be eroded in the process. Your department's past is important for a number of practical reasons:

- It provides a sense of stability and perspective that makes people envision a good career future.

- It is the foundation of a sense of group identity—a cohesiveness of people working toward common goals.

- The past can be a sound basis for current decisions; one can learn the probability of success for many new ideas from a group's unique history.

- It is the source of the work group's reputation within the rest of the organization and among suppliers or customers. These groups bank on your traditional knowledge and expertise.

But all of these values of the past can be rapidly lost if there is a sudden turnover of personnel. Today, there are forces that encourage such turnover: the trend toward early retirement; the lack of stigma in job-hopping; even a deliberate policy of shifting employees around rapidly.

To enjoy the benefits of your work group's past (even if you were not a part of it), consider the following:

- **Make an effort to retain some high-seniority workers.** Sure, you want fresh blood in the group; but if it's all fresh, a sense of direction may be lacking. So make a point of keeping some old-timers around. Offer them incentives like retraining or work restructuring so they can make full use of their vast experience.

- **Demonstrate your own interest in the past.** In this, as in many other facets of your department, your attitude sets the tone for others. If you take the past seriously (by paying attention to old-timers rather than showing irritation with them, for example), others will follow your lead.

- **Institute changes gradually.** Abrupt breaks with continuity unsettle people, and can create work crises. In this sense, respect for the past means not breaking too suddenly with the way things are now, so that today's experience will stay useful tomorrow.

- **Fill in gaps in your own "memory."** If you are a newcomer, find out as much as you can about your department. You might revive some good ideas, or discover some that failed before but might work now under different circumstances.

- ▪ **Observation:** None of this means you should dwell on the past, or use it as an excuse to avoid necessary change. Rather, it means recognizing that the past of your work group is the foundation on which you have to build its future as you continue to function well in the present.

Using Participative Management

An increasing number of CEOs are relying on teams of subordinates to share corporate decision making, according to a Conference Board study. The report finds a trend in "the CEO's utter dependence on a strong executive group. It is underscored by the increasing delegation of authority and a new emphasis on leadership rather than traditional professional management."

For middle managers, this change is significant. Major shifts that start at the top filter down, and the manager who can adapt early will be in a good position when the trend becomes widespread. Even if participative management is not yet evident in your company, there are good reasons to try this management style in your work group:

- Building a strong team of managers can help you respond more effectively to change.

- A team approach helps you meet the challenge of increasing specialization in many business areas by encouraging brainstorming among members with different areas of expertise.
- Participative management feeds your best employees' ambitions and helps you groom successors so you can move up.

Here are some ways to start putting a team together:

- **Adjust your own thinking to leading rather than managing.** That means setting the climate, providing support and inspiration and being the interface between the group and others outside of it. You can work toward this new concept of your role if you have a group of competent people with whom you can share the traditional management functions of control, direction and administration.

- **Analyze subordinates' strengths.** Look at the people who work for you (and with you) with a fresh eye, as though you were about to promote them to more responsible positions. Consider how energetic, imaginative, skilled, knowledgeable, experienced and ambitious each employee really is—and what more he or she might be able to contribute to leading the group.

- **Use individual talents.** As opportunities arise, bring qualified managers in at the inception of a project. Pick those who demonstrate the best potential to deal with a particular area of responsibility, and give them the authority to show what they are able to do in specific situations.

- **Make the most of staff meetings.** If your staff meetings have become perfunctory reporting sessions, try to broaden their focus. Use them to air your concerns and as a vehicle for including the staff in the planning process. Occasionally, encourage project leaders to run segments or entire meetings.

- **Broaden your own horizon.** The more effective the team you develop, the freer you will be to expand your scope of activities. You can start considering the larger organizational or competitive issues of your company and examining ways to make yourself more valuable to it.

Consensus: How to Get It

Decision making by consensus has become a standard administrative procedure in many companies—especially the very competitive high-tech ones where bad decisions can spell quick catastrophe. Nurtured by the case studies and group approaches of the M.B.A. schools, many young managers hesitate to accept any idea that is not presented by a given team.

How does a creative individual operate in a group-dominated environment that is subject only to the force of persuasion? While that person need not become a master of argumentation and debate, he or she should be familiar with some of the techniques passed down by those who have successfully sold their ideas to groups:

- **Understand the decision-making process.** Two professors of psychology—Irving L. Janis of Yale University and Daniel D. Wheeler of the University of Cincinnati—were among the first to define the five stages of the decision-making process: (1) accepting the necessity of a decision ("deciding to decide"), (2) searching for alternatives ("the more the better"), (3) evaluating the options ("focusing on a tentative decision"), (4) committing to a final decision ("planning implementation"), and (5) adhering to the decision ("anticipating setbacks").

  Anyone who has an idea to market would do well to recall Konrad Adenauer's self-challenge: "I insist on being smarter today than I was yesterday." It's impossible to push an idea into policy without all the hard facts and answers and convincing logic you can muster. You must prepare and overprepare and be the best-prepared person in the room: that's a given. And you'll need something else if you want to prevail.

- **Build yourself an image.** Frank Snell, at one time a director of the ad agency Batten Barton Durstine & Osborn and a long-time student of group maneuvering, believes that an image is critical in the decision-making process. "Think about how you project yourself," he advises, "and then set out to develop an image that will support what you have to say, that will make what you say more effective and bring about the changes you want.''

Some specifics: Be neither invisible nor pretentious. Be positive and realistic, strong but not rigid. Above all, don't be a nonstop talker. What kind of person impresses you? Remember the details when you try to shape your image.

- **Be the best listener in the group.** Listening hard will help you spot the selective listeners: people who only hear what they want to hear. Decide whether to bypass these pockets of resistance because they are not listening, or to confront their views with facts they can't ignore.

- **Use some proven persuasive techniques.** For example, recognize that the art of persuasion is a slow and deliberate ritual. Be patient. You can change a person's opinion, but don't expect a quick shift from no to yes. When people do change their minds, they take a very slow route from disbelief to belief. Pace your arguments with a careful balance of fact and emotion.

Check for reruns of the movie classic *12 Angry Men* and watch Henry Fonda gradually bring each juror over to his side. His secret: an awareness that no two people are ever exactly alike. Each has a different point of view and must be convinced differently. This is a *plus*, not a problem for you. It's much easier to take on an individual than a stone wall of unified resistance.

- **Plan how you are going to put your idea into words.** The way we frame our ideas too often says to listeners that we don't know what we're talking about. Frank Snell recommends a formula he calls the 1-2-3 System for presenting ideas:

1. *Statement* (your premise): "I believe this program is going to succeed."

2. *Proof* (facts to prove what you said): "Test samples surpassed our goal."

3. *Restatement* (a reminder of your premise): "I'm convinced we've got a real winner here."

After you've tried all the emotional and factual arguments you can think of, you still have one very effective routine left. Nothing will convince a wavering businessperson more readily than a remark that your idea or some variation of it has been tried before and tried *successfully*. An argument based on ''the reality of success'' is tough to refute.

71

▪ ▪ **Observation:** Managers should never hesitate to confront their peers with new ideas. These are the lifeblood of an organization and their absence can be fatal. Bringing a particular point of view to consensus is known as success.

Strategies for Building a New Team

Your new assignment may sound like a "mission impossible":

— You've been chosen to direct an important new company project, which involves putting together a group comprised of both new and experienced employees.

— You're the manager who has been brought in after a takeover and asked to shape up a department.

— You've survived a merger or reorganization, but your new job— streamlining the department you've been managing—may prove to be an even bigger challenge.

Naturally, you'll feel anxious about building a new staff or department. To proceed with fewer problems, keep your mission in mind and follow these three steps:

Decide Whom You Need

Start by making a list of the various types of specialists needed to get the work done. It's helpful to attach responsibilities to each job so that you can evaluate which staff members have the right experience and skills necessary for the work to be done.

Even more important than credentials is each potential team member's personality, which ultimately has more to do with how well an individual will perform. If, for example, you're trying to build an entrepreneurial environment to make your department more competitive, you'll want to look for employees who aren't afraid to take risks or experiment with different ways of doing things.

When you begin interviewing new candidates or talking with current employees, present scenarios that may come up and ask how they would handle them. Also, decide in advance what the structure of your team will be so that you can explain to each potential staff member how his or her job will relate to other jobs.

Meet With Team Members

Once you've made your selections, talk to people about their goals and find out what resources they need (corporate support, money, equipment) to accomplish them. If their goals are closely related to the team's goals and your staff members feel they have what they need to accomplish them, they'll be more committed to you.

Ask, too, for your staff's ideas on what the potential personnel problems are. If you've brought in outsiders, for example, you may find that seasoned employees are suspicious or fearful about working with them. Tuning into people's feelings in advance can help you defuse anxiety.

You can shorten your team's start-up time by making sure each person is familiar with company procedures and personnel. One way to do that is to assign each person three or four people (on or outside the team) to interview for information vital to their new role. If inexperienced people are part of your team, you can accelerate their learning process by having them work one-on-one with senior staff members.

Establish Communication Procedures

When you first meet with your group, discuss how often and in what manner you'll be talking with one another. If your team members are experienced professionals, ask for their suggestions. Frequent meetings and written reports are a good idea for at least the first three months until team members get to know one another and feel comfortable dealing with each other informally.

Be sure to circulate written information about important things that have been discussed informally—short- and long-term objectives, team member's responsibilities, who reports to whom and deadlines.

■ ■ **Recommendation:** Make it your business to stay on top of the inevitable work-related and interpersonal problems that will surface. Whatever time you spend solving problems now will pay off in greater productivity and a more satisfied team later.

How to Turn Tension
and Conflict Into Action

"The manager's challenge is not to practice management by objectives, but to manage despite diverse objectives," says Dr. Harlan Cleveland, professor emeritus of the Hubert H. Humphrey Institute of Public Affairs (University of Minnesota), and former U.S. ambassador to NATO.

The organization is "a web of tensions," Cleveland observes. "You have people with opposing viewpoints fighting to get them incorporated into executive decisions. Many managers try to lower the tensions that inevitably result. But that's like administering a muscle relaxant. When there is no tension in the muscles, nothing much can happen, and the body falls down." He sees the manager's role as keeping the tension constructive and functional (so that it doesn't boil over into personal animosities).

Cleveland advocates managing with a "next step agenda" that focuses people's attention on immediate action.

For mobilizing dissenting factions, Cleveland suggests:

- **Emphasize the larger need.** Rather than admonishing people to give up their individual viewpoints, remind them of the overall goal and ask them to see their viewpoints in relation to it. Encourage them to match their expertise in their own areas with knowledge of the situation as a whole.

- **Practice unwarranted optimism.** When things are not going well, it's easy to become pessimistic and overly cautious. But it is up to the manager to take some risks despite gloomy predictions, and encourage others to come along.

- **Stress action over ideology.** People must avoid trying to agree on *why* they are agreeing. "If Carter had tried to get Begin and Sadat to reach a philosophical agreement on why they should make peace, the accord never would have been signed," says Cleveland. Too often managers try to get a philosophical agreement before crossing the street together. With a "next step agenda," the manager must be a "get on with it" person who says, "What can we agree to *do* together."

- **Bring hidden dissension to the fore.** People sometimes avoid saying that they disagree. Be suspicious of stalling and sabotaging tactics such as: "Have you gotten a legal opinion?" or "I didn't get the report soon enough" or "It's time for lunch."

Get past procedural questions and ask straight out what is really on the person's mind. Then you will know what action you should take.

The Art of Motivating Employees

U.S. business spends billions annually to rev up workers. In the travel incentive business alone, there are now thousands of service companies that develop and/or run trips to reward employees, as opposed to a few hundred companies a decade ago.

What methods are most used? How can you choose and implement a motivational program that will match your needs and get results? Matt S. Walton III is a managing principal in Los Angeles for Sibson & Co. Inc., a management consulting firm based in Princeton, NJ that develops compensation and incentive programs. He describes the most common types of programs and offers insights and guidelines:

- **Rewards.** Trips, televisions, cash—all can be powerful incentives to pump up performance and boost profits. "Reward programs are especially effective when used with sales and customer service representatives," says Walton. He cautions that, for the reward to be meaningful, it should relate to specific performance measures established in advance. For example, bank personnel might be offered a reward for getting a certain number of customers to buy a CD within a 30-day period.

Reward programs can falter when they are not implemented in the context of employee recognition. Explains Walton: "If handled appropriately, a reward program communicates to employees, 'You are terrific and special because you exceeded expectations. As a token of our appreciation, we are giving you this VCR, vacation or whatever.' If you just hand out prizes, they come to be expected and lose their meaning.''

Walton points out that rewards need to be supported by recognition of each individual's achievements along with appropriate fanfare. Giving employees a plaque and publishing their names in the house organ, for example, can have a greater motivational effect than awarding prizes without the pat on the back that gives them meaning.

- **Guest speakers.** Hiring Fran Tarkenton to kick off a sales convention, or Ken Blanchard to rally first-line managers before a new product introduction, can supply a potent shot of adrenaline. "Over time, managers' pep talks tend to go stale," says Walton. "You can be the most charismatic manager in the world, but when your people hear you saying the same things day in and day out, they tend to turn off. The same message, communicated by a known personality who has earned a reputation for superior performance, can work employees into a heightened state of enthusiasm."

  Lecturers are especially effective as part of a short-term project where it's important to get workers committed. Be aware, however, that the duration of a speaker's impact is actually very short. "The most dynamic personality will leave people on a high for three days at the most," says Walton. Do not expect the speaker to communicate more than one point or theme. If you want someone to explain the complexities of a new strategy, do that yourself.

- **Seminars.** There are two types of motivational seminars: "hard" and "soft." The former motivates employees by communicating quantifiable, practical skills which can be easily translated into on-the-job effectiveness. Examples are "Motivation Techniques for Supervisors" and "Problem Solving, Decision Making and Planning" sponsored by The 1st Seminar Service (88 Middle St., Lowell, MA 01852).

  If you send employees to seminars like these, make sure that the content is consistent with the philosophy and practices of your organization. For example, an employee returning from a seminar on problem solving may set about proposing innovative solutions and suggestions, only to find that the company's managerial mindset discourages exercising such initiative.

  "Soft" programs rely on dynamic or guru-type leaders who attempt to fire up participants with pop psychology terminology and "self-actualization" exercises. "Ninety-eight percent of these seminars are worthless," says Walton. "The leaders are essentially entertainers who convey simple platitudes like, 'If you believe in yourself, you'll be a winner.'"

▪ **Self-instructive programs.** These include books and audio- and videotape programs supplemented by workbooks.

These are especially valuable when you lack the budget for a more elaborate program, says Walton. They can also stimulate an exchange of ideas between you and the employee during which you can motivate the employee directly.

▪ ▪ **Observation:** "When you decide to buy a motivational program, you stand a better chance of getting it approved if you thoroughly research it before presenting the idea to your superiors," advises Walton. Write up your justification for the idea ("to give recognition to the top ten performers"), the desired outcome ("to motivate the team to produce its best so we can double sales"), and specifics on the program, including the name of the consultant(s) you'd like to use and your estimated budget.

Scarce Resources
Can Divide Your Group

It's a basic fact of economic life: scarcity breeds competition. While managers accept this truth in the marketplace, few consider its applicability to members of their own department. In a group that is supposed to be working as a team, a scarcity of resources can breed counterproductive behavior, ranging from hoarding to badmouthing colleagues, to a variety of devious power-grabs.

People faced with inadequate resources often compete for "their" share of whatever is in short supply—access to important information, a good word from you, or even a stack of forms. Cornering the commodity becomes a goal in itself, rather than the means to achieve quality work.

To find out if potential harmful scarcities exist in your operation, consider what resources each group member needs in order to perform well. Begin with the most obvious—workplace furniture and specialized, raw material. Then go on to ask if there is a scarcity of:

- Information about management's short- and long-term goals.
- Feedback on job performance.
- Information about career tracks.
- Competent staff.
- Attention from you.
- Development and training opportunities.
- Time to do each job well.
- Working space.
- Storage space.
- Access to services—e.g., word processing, duplicating, computer time.
- Adequate staff support.
- Information necessary to coordinate work with other groups.
- Invitations to meetings relevant to assigned tasks or projects.

If you answered "yes" to any of these, or you thought of other scarcities not on the list that your department may be suffering, then consider these questions:

- **Is the need real?** Do you and the people working with you really need more of this commodity to get the work out properly, or would something else do instead? If you are short on work space, for example, there is space-saving office furniture on the market that might improve the situation.

- **Is the scarcity reversible?** You may have to start prodding the people who are in a position to end the shortage. Where this means higher costs or budget changes, be prepared to show that the benefits will be commensurate. If you are convincing enough, priorities may be reordered in your favor.

- **What can you do to increase the supply?** It may simply mean reshuffling priorities within your own budget. Other problems may be solved by reorganization (work assignments, service delivery, etc.).

- **How can you best allocate what is scarce?** Some limits are inevitable and those resources that cannot be increased will become your most precious. Try to manage these resources as effectively as possible—allocating them where they promise the greatest pay-off. Perhaps the best example of this is your own time; use it to lead, challenge and reward the people who work for you.

▪ ▪ **Observation:** The availability and allocation of resources will have a direct bearing on the results that you and your team achieve. Analyze them carefully to ensure that the results will be the positive ones you originally set out to obtain.

The Art of Resolving Disputes

Suddenly the air is charged as the voices of two employees rise in a crescendo of anger. Today, one is accusing the other of fouling up the production schedule; yesterday, it was because a customer's order was sent out a day late. Enough is enough. The constant bickering disturbs other workers and upsets the departmental machinery.

Disputes between employees are common and inevitable. The difficult decision is when to step in, says Joseph F. Byrnes, dean of Bentley College Graduate School in Waltham, MA. "Give the warring parties a chance to resolve it on their own," he says. "The time to take action is when things get out of hand and it's affecting their work or disrupting other people's work."

Find out whether the conflict is work-related and has a structural root or whether it is interpersonal and has no relationship to the job or company, advises Byrnes. An interpersonal conflict can happen on or off the job, whereas structural ones are inevitable in many companies.

An easy way to evaluate the conflict, according to Byrnes, is to ask yourself: "If you took these two people out of the situation and put two new people in, would you still have the conflict?" If the answer is yes, it's a structural conflict; if it is no, the cause is definitely interpersonal.

Byrnes points out that structural conflicts can often lead to interpersonal ones. After months—sometimes years—of battling, the two people forget that there are actually systematic reasons for the conflict.

Structural and interpersonal conflicts each can be resolved, says Byrnes, and often the techniques are not so different. First, to resolve a structural conflict:

- **Expand resources.** A work flow problem can often be alleviated by changing the way jobs are scheduled or by providing more resources (or supplies).

- **Clarify job responsibilities.** Conflicts often arise when one department encroaches on another's domain. In engineering companies, for example, designers and engineers often have their differences. The designer creates a product on paper so that the engineer can create the actual product. Inevitably, problems arise when the two professionals are forced to work together to create the working or prototype model. Each one has his or her own ideas about how things ought to be done, hence tempers often flare before solutions are found.

''The manager can step in and redefine who does what in the process and possibly act as a liaison between the two parties,'' explains Byrnes.

Techniques For Dealing With Either Kind Of Conflict

1. **Demand a truce.** Order combatants to stop fighting and work out the problem between themselves. If they're not successful, offer to step in and act as arbitrator. ''They'll often welcome your stepping in because you're lifting the burden of solving the conflict from their shoulders,'' says Byrnes.

2. **Reduce the amount of interaction.** ''Often conflicts cool off when the two parties don't have to speak with each other throughout the day,'' explains Byrnes. ''If they're normally exchanging information all day long, suggest that they meet less frequently, once in the morning and once again in the afternoon. If they're constantly exchanging written information, for example, ask them to give it to a neutral third party who is close by.''

3. **Mediation.** Meet with the parties together. (If it's an explosive issue, it might be better to meet with each one alone in order to gather facts.) Find out what the problem is, thrash it out and work together to find a solution. The process of talking it out can relieve pressure and often defuse the situation.

   Interpersonal conflicts, however, are not that straightforward, he cautions, because they're usually based on irrational differences. One worker, for example, may dislike a colleague because he thinks, feels or acts a certain way. "No matter what the reason (or reasons) behind the disagreement, make it clear that you don't have to like a person to work with him or her. As difficult as they may find it, they must learn to keep their emotions and feelings out of it."

4. **Create common goals.** "Often combatants—whether the cause is structural or interpersonal—fail to see the big picture," says Byrnes. "They concentrate on their particular jobs, which usually represent only one process or part of the company's goals. They lose sight of their roles in the functioning of the entire company. Or they get so wrapped up in their irrational feelings, they miss the important issues before them. By reiterating the company's goals and demonstrating how both employees are vital to the company's success, you might temporarily squelch their anger and create harmony—or at least coexistence." Then you will be able to function effectively on the job.

The Art of Handling Dissent

In any group of employees, you're bound to find some who don't hesitate to speak their minds, even when their opinions conflict with company policy.

This is not inherently good or bad. But you need to learn to distinguish between well-intentioned objections, which contain valid insights, and ill-meant dissent, which tends only to stir up conflict. You must find a place for the former and authority to defuse the latter. Some suggestions:

- **Look for patterns.** Not everyone who states a divergent viewpoint is trying to cause trouble. "Employees tend to build histories of conduct based on consistent intentions," observes Ralph H. Kilmann, professor of business administration at the University of Pittsburgh and author of *Beyond The Quick Fix* (Jossey-Bass Publishing, 350 Sansome St., San Francisco, CA 94104; $25.95). "When someone establishes a track record for taking issue with company policy, that record usually shows a pattern in the way it is expressed. It is not difficult to detect the person's intent through the mode of expression.''

If you see that a person tends to come down hard and strong on company policy, but offers reasonable alternatives and avoids personal attacks, it will be clear that the intent was positive. But if someone repeatedly creates animosity by lying, harassing and accusing, it will become obvious that the intent is not to help the organization but only to achieve personal gain.

The only effective way to deal with this kind of person, says Kilmann, is to issue a strong statement warning the employee that such behavior will not be tolerated.

- **Steer employees' objections to the appropriate time and place.** Certain corporate cultures frown on dissent, however constructive. This need not prevent you from encouraging it within your unit. Just be sure that employees know when and where to speak up. ''Impress on your people the importance of presenting a united front outside of your department,'' advises Kilmann. ''Rather than telling them to suppress their opinions, explain that it could damage the unit if certain outsiders were to perceive disagreement within your group.''

Help your people to recognize those who value dissent and those who see all disagreement as destructive. This will help them to develop the sophistication to complain constructively to the right people.

Don't Be Swayed by Office Politics

Operating procedures are about to be changed to meet a new production schedule. Senior members of your staff favor one solution, the younger ones defend an alternate option. Either one could work.

Each faction is jockeying for power, each wants your support and you are caught in the middle of office politics.

As manager, you want to resolve the situation without offending or alienating either group. ''Uppermost is not being seduced by the politics of one group over another,'' says Dr. Bill Knaus, a management consultant from Longmeadow, MA.

When politics get in the way, it's time to cautiously step in. "You don't want your boss to think that your division is riddled with divisive disputes," he adds. "Your credibility is on the line if you can't right the situation."

Easing tensions between warring factions is not as easy as it sounds. "A bad move on the manager's part could create irreparable barriers, decrease productivity, as well as dampen morale," says Knaus. "The situation must be carefully managed so that you're not taking sides." Your goal is to keep everyone focused on solving a problem and not be sidetracked by personal or political issues.

Sensitive handling involves:

- **Recognizing different factions.** Managers must recognize and respect group differences so they remain objective and are not sidetracked by petty conflicts. "It's only natural that there will be differences of opinion among people with contrasting temperaments, abilities, responsibilities and work styles," says Knaus. "But you can't let these differences be a disruptive force."

- **Being sensitive to people's needs.** "It's also important to understand that people are motivated by different things (money, recognition, power)," Knaus explains. Once you recognize these needs, you'll be better equipped to respond to different factions.

- **Encouraging the factions to sit down and discuss differences.** Set a time limit so that disagreements are resolved speedily. "The manager's job is not to prove anyone right or wrong, but rather to establish a common ground or seek an alternative that best meets the needs of the organization and both groups," says Knaus.

- ■ **Observation:** If an issue is unusually sensitive or complicated, Knaus suggests turning it over to an informed, impartial third party who can act as mediator. This can often be an expedient solution that will leave you in the clear and ensure objectivity.

Three Ways to Gain Allies
in Your Company

Political savvy, handled well, is simply judicious planning in order to benefit fully from one's honest efforts. Take, for example, two office-seekers who visit a day care center. Each places high value on low-cost child care, but one also puts a premium on the right image—she arranges careful press coverage to emphasize her commitment. Guess which politico gets full mileage from the visit?

Some managers, when they think of politics in their organizations, think of game players—those who pull strings and manipulate to get ahead or get even; those who will do whatever is expedient, regardless of the cost to others. But there are managers with integrity *and* political skill who see this skill as an important aspect of management. They agree with Charles de Gaulle's statement: "Politics is too serious a matter to be left to the politicians."

Such managers know that hard work alone is rarely enough to insure the optimum return for your effort. You must have a strategy, work smart as well as hard, use whatever resources are available to advance what you believe in. If this approach sounds as if it might be helpful to you, consider the following factors:

- **It's good politics to give credit.** Your personal success is inter-woven with your people's. One way to see that the people you supervise are on your side is to recognize and showcase their achievements. Accolades—word of mouth, a write-up in the house organ, a memo for the bulletin board, a public thank-you for ex-cellent work—all work toward this end. You might be amazed at the amount of loyalty and commitment to your goals that you can engender in those who realize that you, the boss, appreciate their efforts.

- **Seeking credit is also good politics,** and forthright statements may say it best: an informal meeting with your boss to give an update on impressive sales figures; an announcement at a manager's meeting that pilferage has significantly declined with the installation of the new security system in your department; a quick visit to a supervisor to tell her that you were able to get budget approval for the assistant she requested. Facts speak for themselves—but they may need some amplification to be clearly heard.

- **Alliances are essential.** Cultivating friendly, cooperative relationships with those who have organizational clout can make your cause that much easier to advance. This often means extending yourself socially—throwing a holiday party for colleagues and their spouses, taking a supplier out for drinks, joining a group of department heads at the annual outing rather than sticking with your employees, sending Christmas cards to service staff. It might also mean doing personal or professional favors—giving a summer job to a customer's qualified daughter, traveling to an out-of-town facility in place of an overworked colleague.

Remember to maintain your perspective. Professional friendships and in-company alliances needn't cause you the discomfort of thinking they are phony or superficial, as long as you know them for what they are— more professional than personal. The acid test is to ask yourself: Does this feel natural? Will I regret having done this if it doesn't pay off? Am I enjoying my efforts, or is the only incentive the projected gain? If you are not being yourself, this will have a negative effect on your credibility, while sincerity will be a positive factor.

Refuse To Be Intimidated

You've encountered them: the people who seem to be in total control. They exude self-confidence and—without intentionally doing so—they intimidate you.

Tall people don't mean to intimidate short ones. Men don't always want to intimidate women. Assertive people can't help it if shy ones fade in their presence.

When you must deal with one of those "favored" individuals, something unpleasant often happens. You lose whatever poise and confidence you thought you had. You back off or act foolish—quite unlike your usual self. Your positive self-image self-destructs. How can it be restored?

- **Stop comparing.** "Each of us possesses a complicated array of strengths and weaknesses," says Harvard psychiatrist Dr. William S. Appleton. For example, "You may be more able at numbers and less persuasive with people, but the organization needs both types of workers."

- **Give up on perfectionism.** A rational standard demands that you try your best, not that you never make mistakes, adds Appleton. You make the best of what you have. Remember that the most elegantly turned-out executive will have days when her hair refuses to stay in place or a deal turns sour.

Intimidation by Design

In contrast to no-fault intimidation (the other guy can't help it if he's lucky) is the deliberate kind. The other person may be your boss who is using coercive power on you, or a peer who is undermining you.

The person's Machiavellian tactics (unjust criticism, sarcasm, withholding information, ignoring your ideas) make you feel victimized. "What you must do is 'out-Mac' your opponent," advises Dr. Roy Johnson, professor of psychology at Iowa State University in Ames. Some pointers:

- **Do some self-analysis.** Am I allowing myself to be passive? Why is this person treating me like a doormat? If the individual is on your level, it's important to assess your role in relation to him or her. "See if there is a way to establish some reciprocity between you, some basis for cooperation," suggests Johnson. As colleagues, you need to interact. How does your work affect the other person's?

- **Bring it out into the open.** Unless you confront the intimidator, there can't be any progress. Possibly he or she isn't even aware of the effect on you. But if the intimidation is deliberate, serving notice that you aren't going to be passive about it could go far in squelching it.

- **Learn to be more influential.** The best way to counter intimidation is to develop your own powers. Cultivate your expertise, suggests Johnson. The more competent you are, the greater your confidence to deal with those who would intimidate.

- ▪ **Observation:** Battling intimidation is particularly necessary for executive women who may face a hostile male environment, or minorities who must struggle to get ahead. Wherever there is evidence of deliberate intimidation, it is important to confront it. It is a risk, but one you have to take if there is to be any real growth and security.

Working With Someone You Dislike

No matter what the issue, you can't seem to agree with your colleague about anything. But as managers with equal status in the same company, you have no choice but to work together on projects.

What do you do? Staying at odds and letting the mutual dislike fester just leads to strained nerves. It also makes everyone around you uncomfortable.

The answer—and relief as well—lies in coming to a common understanding and finding a harmonious middle ground.

All disagreements between peers are the result of contrasting work styles, insists Robert Hecht, cochairman of Lee Hecht Harrison, Inc., a New York outplacement firm. "Your work style is a function of your personality," he says. People tend to agree upon broad objectives and goals, but disagree on how to reach those goals.

To reconcile differences, Hecht offers these suggestions:

- ▪ **Appreciate your colleague's opinion.** While you may not agree with another person's approach or style, respect the fact that it also has value. Also, try to see issues within a perspective and don't blow them out of proportion.

- ▪ **Depersonalize your differences.** Don't fall into the trap of attacking the person. Stick to relevant issues and put emotions aside. Question facts, but not motives.

  During a critical disagreement, Hecht advises standing back:

  —Allow the other person to react. Hear what he or she has to say without letting your feelings interfere.

  —Work toward agreement on what the work problem is. After you have both stated your opinion, develop a joint definition you can both address.

—Test your solutions. Give yourself a time period, 60 to 90 days, for example, to monitor a program to see if it works. Then you can fine-tune it and make adjustments based on real-life experience.

▪ ▪ **Observation:** By working closely together and having an ongoing dialogue concerning how goals are to be reached, you're also breaking down barriers. This will help you reach a better understanding of your colleague's work style.

When a Colleague
Steps on Your Toes

An aggressive sales manager in your division attempts to get the better of you by resorting to one or more of these tactics:

- Trying to lure away some of your best salespeople.
- Prospecting in your territory.
- Undermining your ability as a manager.
- Using your contacts to get new customers.

Both of you want the same things: to chalk up exemplary production records, power, money and better perks. The disturbing difference is that you're playing fair while your colleague is employing unsavory tactics.

It's a common problem that crops up in all companies, regardless of the industry involved. Solving it can be difficult, says Raphael Amit, associate professor of management at the Kellogg Graduate School of Management at Northwestern University. "But it can be righted tactfully and diplomatically," he says. "One thing is certain: The problem can't be ignored because it's not going to go away. Trying to live with the inequality is not recommended because problems will only escalate."

Almost always, the answer is constructive confrontation. An aggressive, hostile or retaliatory approach seldom works. Consider the following strategy proposed by Amit:

▪ **Make an appointment to talk,** preferably on neutral ground away from the office (maybe a long lunch or dinner after work). Face to face, your colleague can't evade the issue by taking phone calls or running out to other appointments.

- **You need not tell this person the reason for the get-together.** If he or she thinks it's just an informal business chat, the person won't be heavily armed with excuses.
- **Prepare yourself.** Don't walk in cold. Make a list of everything you want to discuss and commit it to memory.

The Meeting

- **Get straight to the point.** Put all your cards on the table. "For the past six months, you have undermined my ability to some of my customers and employees. I've also heard from several old customers that you're trying to horn in on my territory."
- **Don't get angry.** It will be difficult, but you must keep your emotions in check and deal calmly with this person.
- **Be prepared for outraged reaction followed by denial.** Counter calmly with evidence. Mention names and dates, if this is at all possible.
- **Neutralize the conflict with a solution.** Once you've presented the facts and issues, work toward a solution. Make it clear that you're not a threat and that you're not standing in this person's way. He or she may not realize that things can be worked out satisfactorily. If it's a territorial dispute, create guidelines and boundaries. "Our territories are large, there is plenty of room for both of us." Stress that you're both in this together and that you want the same things. Work toward peaceful coexistence.

If you can't resolve the dispute yourself, your last resort is speaking to your boss. But it's a dangerous alternative that could backfire, warns Amit. Territorial disputes may be easy to resolve, but most others may pose problems if the boss doesn't want to get involved. You may be putting your boss in an awkward position. "He or she may think you're incapable or resolving your own affairs, and you could wind up alienating this important person," says Amit. "Don't assume that your boss can magically solve this problem. Ideally, it's best if you do it."

Don't Let Yourself Be Seduced
by Kindness

A talented associate has left and all his projects have been turned over to one of your colleagues, with whom, until now, you've had only indirect dealings.

During a casual conversation with her, you deplore the loss of your associate and express the hope that the firm won't suffer. Your colleague compliments you on your concern, says she finds your high standards admirable, and then asks you to expand upon and check some technical material in one of your ex-associate's projects.

Dilemma: You're overburdened and resent the request. If you refuse—after having been told how wonderful you are—you might insult your colleague.

Before you say anything you might regret later, take a moment to think and ask yourself:

- **Why me?** Your colleague may feel threatened by you and could be making a power play. Trying to pressure you into doing extra work is one way to put you in your place.

   The other possibility is that she is in over her head and in a panic, and knows you can be counted on to do what's necessary.

   Be guided by what you know about this individual from the past and by your own intuition as well.

- **What if I say no?** Are you really jeopardizing the organization by declining? Probably not. Your colleague will have to find a way to have this work done or her head will be on the block, since the project is now her responsibility. Saying no lets the person know that, despite her flattery, you're not an easy touch.

- **Can I say yes, conditionally?** If you have reason to believe that the work will be done in a slipshod way, then you might want to take it on. But you can say, "I'm willing to help out this time, but I'm swamped myself—so don't count on me for next time," Then make sure your boss knows of your additional contribution.

■ ■ **Observation:** It's easy to be lulled by flattery. And there's something cozy and tempting about the attitude that "We're all in this together." But don't let yourself be seduced into a reluctant submission.

Defending Yourself
Against Verbal Bullies

Remember the schoolyard bully who waited in the shadows so he could throw your books in a puddle?

As adult managers, we don't have to worry about being waylaid by physical bullies at work. Instead, we sometimes have to contend with putdowns and innuendoes from tyrannical bosses or senior managers.

"It's like being hit in the stomach with a fist of words," explains Suzette Haden Elgin, author of *The Gentle Art of Verbal Self-Defense*. (Sold by direct mail, Barnes & Noble Book Store, Dept. G.A., 126 Fifth Ave., New York, NY 10011; $6.95 plus $1.00 shipping/insurance.) "Verbal bullying is very much like physical bullying. Instead of physical force, language is used to inflict damage." Forget the cliché about sticks and stones. Adds Elgin, "Words can hurt you."

▪ **Why do verbal bullies resort to shooting nasty barbs?**
   1. It's often a game and a traditional way of dealing with others.
   2. People get a sadistic kick out of it.
   3. Someone above the abuser may be doing it to him or her. The victim takes it out on the next person in the pecking order.

▪ **What might a verbal bully say?**
   • "If you *really* wanted to get ahead in this company, you'd turn in your reports on time."
   • "Don't you *even care* that our sales levels are plunging?"
   • "You call yourself a manager."
   • "Everyone *knows* why you can't get along with your staff."
   • "*Even you* should be able to understand that our competitors are practically at our doorstep."

▪ **How do you deal with the verbal bully?** Punching the person out is not going to get you very far. Instead, take action and short-circuit the attacker, advises Elgin.

91

Analyze the verbal assault. The first part of each sentence contains a negative presupposition ("If you *really* wanted to get ahead" implies that you are a shiftless no-good). The second part of each sentence is a direct accusation which Elgin calls the bait.

If you respond to the bait, you are accepting the negative supposition and you are in for a fight—just what the bully wanted.

Every verbal attack has two parts: what the abuser expects you to go for and what always gets you in trouble (the bait), and the real attack (the presupposition). Always respond to the real attack.

Example: "If you *really* wanted to get ahead in this company, you'd turn in your reports on time." If you respond by saying, "What do you mean? I always get my reports in on time," you've fallen for the bait. What you should respond to is "If you *really* wanted to get ahead." Answer by asking, "When did you start thinking I don't care about succeeding in this company?" By refusing the bait and responding neutrally to the real attack, you defuse your attacker and stop him in his tracks. That's not a reply he expected. If you keep cool and address the unfair presupposition, you gain control of the situation.

In general, overlook the bait and respond to the presupposition with something neutral. It will throw the verbal bully off balance and save you from an exhausting argument.

▪▪ **Observation:** You don't have to let a verbal bully boss ride herd on you and make your life miserable. Don't fall into a victim role, warns Elgin. Most verbal victims are not aware that they're feeding bullies. Step away from the problem so you can analyze it and then squelch it calmly before it really gets out of hand.

Deception and Those Who Practice It

— An employee says, "I had nothing to do with it. I don't know anything about it." However, a reliable source reports that he was the prime instigator.

— An employee tells you, "The project is coming along beautifully. No problems." Your secretary tells you he hasn't even opened the file yet.

— One of your salespeople reports that a potential customer has responded enthusiastically to her sales pitch and "plans to sign a contract very soon." You happen to run into the potential customer and learn that his response was lukewarm and that he has signed with a competitor.

"Employees attempt to deceive their bosses for several basic reasons," notes Ronald C. Pilenzo, president and chief operating officer of the Society for Human Resource Management in Alexandria, VA:

- **Personal gain and recognition.** This is often tied to competitiveness, where people try to surpass co-workers or cover themselves against competitive maneuvers.

- **Revenge or sabotage against co-workers or bosses.** This occurs when an employee harbors a deep-seated resentment of his or her work situation.

- **Strain due to personal problems,** such as family tension or financial pressures.

- **Self-protection** because of a fear of being perceived as inadequate to the demands of the job.

The forms of deception vary. There are pathological liars who lie and deceive in an almost compulsive way. Other individuals selectively calculate when, where and how to use dishonesty. Still others are not actually conscious that they are lying. They may cover up or exaggerate the facts when they are under stress and may not be aware that they are practicing deception.

Regardless of its roots, the problem can be effectively dealt with through the use of the following steps:

- **Approach it as a performance issue.** "If you confront an employee on his or her deceptive behavior, you run the risk of incurring a lawsuit for defamation of character, preventing advancement or unjust dismissal," warns Pilenzo. Therefore, he advises, it is important to look at the behavior from the standpoint of how it affects the person's overall performance. Then you can focus your discussion accordingly.

- **Deal with each instance as it occurs.** It's easy to tell yourself, "I'll speak to her about this at her next performance appraisal," or "We're very busy now. This can wait until next week." A dangerous approach, says Pilenzo. "If you store things up, the employee will either deny that it happened or claim not to remember.''

- **Confront the person in a nonaccusatory manner.** A good way to start the discussion is with something like: ''There seems to be a problem here. I am not accusing you, but I've discovered that the costs were greatly lower than what was reported to the client. Can you tell me what's going on?''

    When put on the spot, the employee may admit to having lied. If so, the following steps are essential:

- **Issue a warning.** Avoid the temptation to soften the blow with vagaries. Says Pilenzo: ''State unequivocally that if the behavior continues, the employee's job will be in jeopardy.'' Follow up the discussion with a written warning in the form of a memo addressed to the employee.

- **State that you are keeping documentation.** ''Tell the employee that you are recording the specifics of the event and of the discussion, in a memo to his or her file,'' advises Pilenzo. ''Include dates, names and all the particulars.'' Such documentation is essential, should a lawsuit ensue.

- **Offer assistance.** The assistance might take several forms: setting up weekly meetings to discuss the problem that led to the deceit; calling a joint meeting with any other individual whose behavior may have influenced the dishonesty; or, in the event that you suspect an underlying personality disorder or personal problem, referring the employee to counseling.

- ■ **Observation:** If you note a pattern of deceit, it may be appropriate to examine your own actions; you may be doing something that precipitates dishonesty. Could you, for example, be communicating unrealistic expectations or setting impossibly high standards? Could you be so intolerant of error that employees find it easier to lie than to endure your wrath? Ask someone you trust for an objective assessment. Then take an honest look at yourself and start to deal with the problem as you see fit.

Dealing With Backstabbing

Like desperate survivors in a lifeboat, managers whose jobs are jeopardized because of company change sometimes resort to tactics they wouldn't ordinarily consider.

One of the worst—backstabbing—often increases during a stormy period, but it can occur even in a normal business climate. It pays to be on the lookout for colleagues or superiors who may be out to undermine you so that you can decide when and how to respond.

Motives. Backstabbers' actions are often triggered by several different things, rather than one particular factor. A sense of insecurity, which may be heightened during a period of transition, is most often the reason why someone tries to discredit you. You may exude an air of competence that the underminer perceives as threatening. Or your responsibilities may overlap territory the backstabber regards as his— or hers—alone.

During a restructuring, you may in fact be a real threat to someone who is willing to resort to devious means to get rid of you. Even in stable companies, healthy competition among peers for the few top management spots can turn sour. Finally, someone may be out to get you because you inadvertently said or did something that was misinterpreted.

Tactics. Backstabbing is like guerilla warfare—the enemy's actions are often invisible, but the results aren't. One of the most common tactics is badmouthing. It can happen in meetings when an enemy says something disparaging about you—but neither you nor an ally are there to dispute it. Clever backstabbers often badmouth their victims to superiors who are their allies. The information is then often passed along from a ''neutral'' source to your mutual boss.

Spreading rumors about your work or your personal life is another favorite strategy of backstabbers. But they run the risk of digging their own corporate graves if they're found out to be the source.

Sabotage is another tactic. Backstabbers have been known to steal mail and memos, scramble computer disks, change important times on computerized calendars, and fail to pass along important messages.

Backstabbers can also create roadblocks to your doing a good job. They may withhold critical information, sit on reports you submit, or even try to set you back by pointing out flaws in your work to important people.

Remedies. Once you realize that someone is trying to undermine you, analyze the situation before reacting. The first time a backstabber attacks, you may be better off ignoring it, especially if the stakes aren't that great. The advantage of letting your work speak for itself and appearing unflustered is that the backstabber may retreat because you haven't provided any fuel for the conflict. On the other hand, the person may perceive you as being cowardly and escalate the mischief.

When the stakes *are* great, or the backstabber's actions are damaging, it's best to confront him or her, preferably in private. You don't have to make accusations. It's often sufficient to let the individual know that you're aware of what's going on. You might say, "Someone has been saying untrue things about my work. I don't know who it is, but if you hear anything, I'd appreciate your letting me know." If you deliver the same message to others, it's likely that you'll neutralize the backstabber's actions because others are likely to catch on to his or her tactics.

Confronting someone directly can be effective if this individual has made no attempt to hide his or her campaign. But threatening to go to your mutual boss is likely to backfire. A backstabber can defuse this by telling your boss, "Joe thinks I'm out to get him." Then when you do come in with a complaint, your boss may question whether it's legitimate.

Defending yourself to management, in any event, should be done carefully. It's in your best interest to be cool and to have objective proof of the backstabber's ploys in hand. If you don't, you're better off alerting management that someone is undermining you, that it's not doing you or your staff any good, and to let you know if they hear where it's coming from.

■■ **Observation:** The best preventive measure you can take is to make allies who are likely to alert you to potential underminers or defend you against detractors on an ongoing basis. You will find that this is a wise precaution to take.

Badmouthing
Cannot Always Be Ignored

One line of management thinking has it that all employees can be won over eventually with the right word or the right action. And, in many cases, that will indeed turn out to be true. There are times, however, when a lot of real turmoil is going on just beneath the apparently calm surface.

Take this situation one Boston manager finds herself in. "I have one employee who acts very friendly to my face," she writes, "but other people tell me that he is always trying to undermine what I say or do. For example, he'll say things like, 'She should never have handled it that way,' or 'I don't think she should have given him that bonus.' This goes on not only with the employees in my department, but also with people in management. How can I confront this individual without betraying others?"

The "talk" that this manager describes is the type that can be bothersome to some managers—particularly those newly promoted. Many managers would ignore it. Nevertheless, allowing oneself to be undermined would be a mistake for any manager. This is why, depending on the situation, it may be essential to come up with answers to some to-the-point questions . . .

- **Who is doing the talking?** The employee may be a typical malcontent, always sounding off about something. Or he or she may be someone whose job performance is never quite up to par, never really getting anywhere. If so, chances are that others in the group won't pay much attention to those attempts to undermine you. On the other hand, if the employee is fairly solid and has a certain amount of clout, it's time to be aware.

- **Who is doing the listening?** Is the message being heard only by some people in the group—or are they all tuned in to it? Is it reaching outside the confines of the department? The more people listening, the wider the scope of the problem.

- **Who is telling you?** Reasonable prudence means that you can't always take everything you hear at face value. It could well be that the people who are informing you about these undermining attempts are reporting honestly, out of concern for the overall good of the operation. But there is always the possibility that they are reporting for some less cooperative reason—exaggerating the situation in an attempt to win favor or even cause problems for someone else.

Answers to the foregoing questions won't be easily found. But with some careful observation on your part and some discreet questioning of people you trust, you should be able to arrive at some valid conclusions. If you decide that action must be taken, here's how you might handle matters:

- **Make a point of publicizing the reasons behind what you say and do.** Though this isn't always possible, in many cases you can spread the word up and down the line. Too many managers ignore this approach—they simply present *faits accompli* that leave people wondering about the reasons why they were done. This is fertile soil for resentment, false rumors, sub rosa accusations. But if you explain the whys and wherefores, and people understand your reasoning, you provide little ammunition for the second guessers.

- **Have a low-key discussion with the employee in question.** There's no need to mention any names or betray any informants. Just cut to the heart of the matter . . . "It has come to my attention that you are not in agreement with several things I've done recently. Would you like to tell me why." This gives the employee a chance to air any legitimate grievances—and there may be some, if only through a lack of understanding.

You might then continue on an up-beat note . . . "I'm glad we talked about this and in the future, if you don't agree with something, why don't you come and discuss it with me? I'm always interested in useful ideas."

Will this approach solve the problem? It may. Often, employees talk against a manager because they are dissatisfied with some aspect of their job or they feel that they are not getting enough recognition or attention. A chance to participate more, to know the manager better, could easily put an end to all the undermining that's taking place.

Should this not prove to be the case, well, you've made it clear that you're aware of what's going on and that stringent measures can certainly be expected if your warnings go unheeded in the future.

Spotting and Handling Manipulators

— An account executive negotiating for a raise dishonestly implies that she has a more lucrative job offer.
— A secretary campaigning for a word processor plays her bosses against each other, inaccurately portraying them as more enthusiastic than they actually are.
— A shop steward threatens to file grievances over petty issues, with the underlying motive of getting the manager to reassign him.

These are some examples of ways in which some employees may attempt to manipulate their managers.

Manipulation is an effort to influence circumstances and gain benefits through dishonest and/or unfair means, explains George Bell, a management consultant in Westborough, MA. Employees most often try to pressure or dupe managers into disclosing information, making a favorable decision or committing themselves to stretching the rules against their better judgment.

"Manipulators are usually people who, as children, learned that they could get what they wanted from parents and teachers by lying and scheming," Bell notes. "As adults, they rely on the same techniques, rather than risk the less familiar methods of honest, forthright communication."

Bell warns that managers can inadvertently perpetuate manipulation. "Some techniques are so subtle that managers are unaware that they are being manipulated," he says. "They respond as the employees want, thereby encouraging them."

If allowed to continue, manipulation sets off a chain of counterproductive events: The manipulators find that scheming is effective, so they continue. Employees looking on lose respect for the manager who fails to see through the ploys or to end them. Seeing that dishonesty is rewarded, the observers tend to feel demoralized. Often the best people leave; others just stop caring about their work. Some onlookers see that manipulation gets results, so they adopt the same techniques.

Bell describes some common methods of manipulation and suggests responses:

- **Bandwagon technique.** The employee says or implies that "everybody" does something a certain way. It's an attempt to get you to join an often nonexistent crowd by making you feel as though you're wrong for being different in your approach.

  Suggestion: Close the case. "The natural reaction is to try to justify your stance," notes Bell. "But by taking a defensive posture, you are asking to be manipulated." Once you have issued a considered decision, don't get involved in negotiations. A good response: "That may be true for others, but we're doing it this way here."

- **"Always" technique.** Example: "You always give the good assignments to her." The manipulator seizes control of the discussion by subtly prodding you to respond to some general accusations.

  Suggestion: Demand specifics. Start by asking, "What do you mean by always?" and continue questioning until you get to the person's real concern. By forcing the person to be literal, you take away all of his or her ammunition. You also put the employee in a responsive position, and thereby take control of the discussion.

- **Threats.** This is an extreme tactic designed to intimidate you. The manipulator sees you as a pushover and may threaten to go over your head, resign or disclose embarrassing information about you.

  Suggestion: Stand firm. Bell suggests the "broken record" technique, where you simply repeat your position, refusing to waver. He adds: "Only managers who doubt their own judgment give in to threats."

- **Subversive techniques.** Employees may try to control your actions by purposely making you look bad or holding up production. Their methods include spreading rumors and "overlooking," "losing" or "forgetting" things intended to cause you embarrassment or lost time.

  Suggestion: Consider disciplinary measures. When enforced fairly and consistently, reprimands and warnings let employees know that they will be penalized for these devious, unprofessional tactics.

- **Card stacking.** The employee presents information that supports an issue while omitting opposing facts.

  Suggestion: Reserve judgment. If you are unfamiliar with the subject, or suspect that you are not being given the full story, say: "I'll look into it and get back to you."

By a Jury of Their Peers

"Employees now feel they can get a square deal," says William Blake. "Before, they felt the deck was stacked against them." What has made the difference at the Borg-Warner plant in Bellwood, IL, where Blake was human resources manager before his retirement, is a peer review system for handling employee grievances.

Under this system, a disgruntled employee takes a complaint to a panel composed of other employees plus members of management. The panels are usually made up of three to six people, with the peers always in the majority. A complainant may bring a fellow employee or someone from personnel to help at a hearing, but not an outside attorney. After listening to the employee and his or her supervisor, the panel votes by secret ballot, and its decision is binding.

Employee members of the panel are chosen at random, by the complainant, from a pool of volunteers who usually receive a full day's training before joining the pool. At Borg-Warner, 70 out of the 1,200 employees at the site have been trained. Independent consultant Harvey S. Caras (of Caras & Associates, Columbia, MD), who sets up peer group systems within companies, says that training includes "how the system works, what questions panel members should or should not ask, listening skills, legal considerations such as the right to privacy, and how to deal with feedback in the plant."

Caras, who is credited with having formalized the peer review procedures when he was employee relations manager for General Electric's appliance plant in Columbia, MD, says each company determines what power its panel will have. But usually the panel cannot change rates of pay, benefit plans or work rules. Panels typically handle such cases as discipline, suspension or termination, or performance appraisal. The role of the panel is essentially to evaluate a decision and determine whether or not it was fair.

The Practice Is Spreading

Peer review was instituted at Honda of America in Marysville, OH. It helps employees understand that management decisions are well-founded and not issued "just because a manager woke up on the wrong side of the bed that morning," says an employee relations coordinator who has worked with the method.

At Honda, where peer review is used only to adjudicate cases of separation or termination, any employee who works in production, has at least one year of service with the company, and has not needed any management counseling within the preceding 12 months is eligible to serve on the panel.

The coordinator says peer review gives employees a better understanding of what management does and also ensures that management doesn't "jump the gun" when deciding to terminate an employee. He stresses, however, that "when a person violates a company policy and it is a separation-of-employment offense, we don't base our decision on whether or not we'd win" in front of a panel.

A much broader employee spectrum is involved in peer review at Public Service of New Mexico, in Albuquerque: office, professional, and technical people, everyone from senior-level engineers down to entry-level clerical people. Panels handle "anything that doesn't set policy," says Randy Helton, former manager of human resources programs. In one case, an employee who was dissatisfied with her performance appraisal went to peer group review, which ruled in her favor.

An Important Benefit

Helton says peer review was instituted when there were heavy layoffs because of a "general contraction of our overall business," and management wanted to give people a chance to appeal if they were laid off. Very few cases have actually come before the panels, he says, because "no one likes the publicity and so there is an impetus for people to take care of their problems themselves." That is actually one of the major benefits of having the program set firmly in place.

More and more companies are installing the peer review system. Caras has installed nearly 40 programs, including several at General Electric and Borg-Warner locations and a Michelin Tire facility in Canada. He says it is possible that there are as many as 100 programs in place because a number of companies have proceeded to set up programs on their own.

Doing It Right

Borg-Warner's Blake, who says, "I haven't seen a drawback yet," to the system, cautions against trying to do it on your own. As enthusiastic as managers are about peer review, they all stress that it will work only if it is properly set up and then taken seriously by management. Abuses of the system must always be avoided.

THE POLITICS
OF LEADERSHIP

When Others Presume
on Your Friendship

"This kind of thing is new to me," writes a manager who has recently gone from being a professional employee to the head of her own department, "so I'm sort of feeling my way. What concerns me at the moment is establishing the right atmosphere and tone. I certainly don't want to come across as a tyrant—I've run into one or two of those in my career. But I've also seen people who were too easy-going, too informal—and that particular style didn't work very well either.

"Is there a fine line I should walk between the two? I want to get along well with people, but I also have to make sure that the work gets done efficiently and effectively. Any ideas on how I could go about doing both?"

Organizational style, these days, tends to be more informal—which is usually an advantage: The atmosphere is more relaxed, communication barriers are reduced, problems surface more quickly and easily. Concern and cooperation are also more readily offered.

Informality can be stretched too far, however, and this can cause difficulties for the person in a supervisory position. People may ask for special favors, for example, or shrug off criticism. The atmosphere may become so relaxed that productivity starts to slow down.

The question, then, for anyone in a position like the above manager's, is how can you gain the advantages of an informal style while not crossing over into too much informality? Here are some answers:

- **Proceed with caution.** For anyone who is just taking over supervisory responsibilities, the best approach is to move *slowly*. Give the situation a little time, assess the people you will be working with, be alert to the signals they send when you question them, assign work and so on. And lean toward a more formal approach as you're sizing things up. It's a lot easier to go from formal to informal than it is the other way around.

- **Remember that you don't have to be a friend.** This is something that people who are new to managerial responsibilities often fail to take into consideration. In their desire to be liked, they go too far with the friendship approach, and this ultimately hampers their ability to give directions, or offer justifiable criticism, or make unpleasant decisions.

  Actually, trying to act as if everyone is your friend won't help you do your job any better. A relationship can be businesslike and matter of fact—and still be productive.

- **Let work be the primary topic of conversation.** This doesn't rule out casual conversation, of course—that's an essential part of building a relaxed atmosphere. But your main purpose, after all, is to make sure that the work gets out. So don't hesitate to tell employees what's expected of them, explain procedures, ask questions, share organizational news, listen to problems, be ready with encouragement when the going gets tough. All this can be done informally, but in a way that clearly indicates that work is the number one concern.

- **Be comfortable in your role.** Undoubtedly, there will be times when you have to use pressure or exert your authority. You will have to criticize, evaluate performance, make a decision that is difficult for others to accept. But if you have been fair and even-handed in the past, your remarks and decisions are likely to be accepted, in spite of any initial grumbling that takes place.

  There may be times, too, when you have to convey instructions or directives from someone up the line which no one, including yourself, thinks are sensible or justified. In situations of this kind, it can be tempting to disassociate yourself from the whole thing with an it's-none-of-my-doing approach. But if you take that path, your employees may think you're currying their favor, and that really won't do much for your image.

  If you don't like a particular directive, discuss the matter with your boss and try to enlist his or her help in getting it changed. In the meantime, you might alert others to what you have done, with an explanation that the directive must be followed until any change is made. Again, this can be done in an informal manner—a back-and-forth exchange of ideas and suggestions might provide you with added ammunition for your fight.

•• **Observation:** One of the benefits of a more informal style is that in an open, relaxed atmosphere, you are much more in touch with what is really going on. People feel free to discuss problems. They are also quicker to propose ideas of their own and more receptive to suggestions from you. Basically, it's a matter of treating people like adults—so that they respond in kind.

The Masculine Mystique About Managing Women

Even the most fair-minded male executives are sometimes guilty of unintentional discrimination against women on their staff, according to a study undertaken by Catalyst, a national research and advisory organization. The reason: Male managers' perceptions of women are often based on traditional cultural values rather than current work and family realities.

"One result is that men and women feel uncomfortable dealing with each other, and that can lead to communication and productivity problems," says Lisa Hicks, a senior associate at Catalyst, New York, NY. Here are some of the most typical situations in which men's well-intentioned behavior can backfire and how you can reduce the possibility of having it affect you and your female staff members:

▪ **Awarding promotions and relocating.** Given two equally qualified people, one male and one female, managers often assume that the male is the better risk because he is more likely to put career rather than family considerations first. That assumption is not necessarily valid. There are women who will make sacrifices for their careers and men who will put their families ahead of their work.

Before you rule out a female candidate, make sure that you know what her ambitions and level of commitment are. If women who work for you haven't articulated their priorities, ask about them. It's also important that your female staff members be aware of what's necessary for advancement so that they can decide what they are—and are not—willing to do.

▪ **Performance feedback.** Some managers find it difficult to give women honest criticism because they're worried that women will react emotionally—and perhaps even cry. Realize first that unless a person knows what her weaknesses are, she won't be able to improve; so you're effectively denying her the right to advance. Second, keep in mind that crying is as valid an emotional response as anger, and that there is no evidence to support the assumption that women cry more often than men in office situations. Finally, if a person you're critiquing gets upset, you can always say "Let's take a break," and allow the person to collect herself or, as some consultants suggest, pass her a tissue and then continue the discussion.

- **Travel.** When overnight or extensive travel is required, managers often send male staff members because they assume—often subconsciously—that mothers should be at home with their children and wives with their husbands, or that travel isn't safe for single women. These assumptions work against female staff members since travel can provide valuable job experience. Again, the best policy is to ask women on your staff what their preferences are and to let them know the type of experience they might gain before you rule out the possibility of sending them on business trips.

To find out if your polite and proper behavior may in fact be resented by the women you manage, you need to analyze your own reactions in different situations. Talk to female colleagues and staff members to learn about their perceptions of your attitudes.

If you find that you do treat women you manage differently, that insight alone may change things. It will certainly make you more sensitive to your own prejudices and how they affect others. And you probably will consider your decisions about female staff more carefully.

Racial Conflicts on the Job

The workplace is becoming more racially diverse, thanks to affirmative action and increased educational opportunities for minorities. Unfortunately, racial tensions often manifest themselves. These can disrupt working relationships, slow down productivity, dampen motivation, alienate clients and customers, and even invite legal action.

When racism erupts, managers tend to make some common mistakes, like:

— **Setting ultimatums.** "Some managers simply say, 'You two will work together or else,'" says Maudine Cooper, staff director for the District of Columbia government mayor, Washington, DC. "This approach only makes matters worse." Forcing a relationship does not change people's feelings, which are at the root of the problem. As long as they continue to harbor the hatred or mistrust or whatever it is they feel, the problem will tend to persist.

— **Automatically taking sides.** Some managers blame the person who is not of their own race, without bothering to find out exactly what is going on. Others automatically take the side of the minority person, on the assumption that minorities are *always* the ones discriminated against. Neither practice is fair.

— **Ignoring, downplaying or making light of the problem.** Not every minor incident warrants a major conference. But it is important to note what has happened and to let the individuals involved know that you are aware of it. In the case of a serious incident, it is shortsighted, unrealistic and also dangerous to ignore it in hopes that it will go away by itself.

"Sometimes a manager will make light of an incident or even joke about it," comments George Davis, a human resources consultant and co-author with Gregg Watson of *Black Life in Corporate America* (Doubleday, 666 Fifth Ave., New York, NY 10103; $7.95 paper). "An incident that seems inconsequential to the manager may have had a major impact on one of the people involved."

He adds that when employees feel that their manager does not take their problems seriously, they may express their resentment through passive-aggressive tactics, causing productivity and morale to suffer.

— **Overreacting.** "Some managers go to extremes and actually fire people, take disciplinary action or transfer employees to other departments or offices" explains Davis. "Ultimately, this creates more problems than it solves."

Adds Cooper: "The manager may wind up with a group all of one race and that broadcasts the message that people of other races need not apply. It may also bring an individual discrimi-

111

nation suit.'' According to Cooper, these suits—where one person within an organization, rather than the employer, is sued—are currently on the rise.

Suggestions for Handling Flare-ups

- **Call in a counselor.** Many large organizations have people on staff who are trained to deal with racial issues in a sensitive and objective manner. ''The counselor should meet with both parties, even if only one is obviously at fault,'' stresses Cooper. Contact your human resources department and ask if someone can sit down with the individuals involved to help them work things out.

- **Use outside training programs.** Seminars are a second choice, since they cannot provide the same individualized attention and lack an insider's understanding of your organization. But, if there is no one internally, your employees may benefit from one of the many seminars designed to teach skills for working together harmoniously.

- **Provide incentives.** ''It is difficult to change people's prejudices,'' says Cooper. ''But you can get them to change the way they act.'' One sound way, she says, is to include evaluations of EEO compliance in supervisors' performance reviews.

- ▪ **Observation:** As a leader, your own sensitivity in dealing with people of other races is bound to filter down to your employees. ''Make an effort to understand the social forces that motivate and inspire employees of other races,'' advises Davis.

  There are plenty of ways to find out about other people: periodicals aimed at specific groups, books, plays, films, dance. Adds Davis: ''It's essential to deepen your understanding of issues important to each culture so that you can better appreciate your employees' needs and sensitivities.''

One Promotion, Two Candidates

An important slot has been created to meet the demands of an increased workload. You have two subordinates who are contenders for the position. How do you choose the right one? It's a tricky situation. A wrong move could create tension or even animosity between candidates. You must be discreet and tactful in approaching the choice.

Most important in making the decision is objectivity. It's quite natural to have personal preferences based on capability. The difficult part is putting your feelings aside so you can pick the right person for the job based on the candidates' specific qualifications.

As you appraise each candidate, look at the organization as a whole and determine which person can meet its new needs.

Which candidate is more comfortable in the current corporate culture? If the company is in a steady growth phase, for example, which person is more likely to make significant contributions? Which is more adaptable, flexible, assertive and growth-oriented? Conversely, if the company is taking enormous risks and entering a precarious period earmarked by unknown hazards, which candidate is more entrepreneurial? Who can best cope with and overcome insecurity?

Next, look at the specific job requirements and measure each of the candidates against them. Analyze the skills necessary for the job to see how each contender stacks up on scientific, technical, organizational, logistical/analytical and supervisory skills, among many others.

No less important are the personal qualities, such as the ability to get along with others and the enthusiasm to create a productive climate, that the new position will certainly require.

When you've made your choice, keep in mind that it's a judgment call based upon carefully weighing who can best meet the criteria for the job. Things could go badly at first. Be prepared to offer support. You might modify the job specifications so the chosen person can more easily adapt to his or her new responsibilities in the beginning.

- ▪ ▪ **Observation:** Don't forget the loser. Chances are this candidate knew that promotion was a possibility. You owe this person an honest explanation of why someone else got the job and what the future may bring. The candidate might not have the qualifications for the particular position, but possesses valuable skills that you see leading in other directions. If you fear losing this person, it is time to try job enrichment. Broaden the individual's responsibilities with more challenging projects and a pay raise if possible, to soften the blow.

Are Formal Performance Appraisals Enough?

If your company has a formal employee appraisal system, do you feel that:

- A high rating will boost an employee's enthusiasm for the organization?
- A satisfactory rating will provide a motivating push for better work?
- An unsatisfactory rating will provide a motivating push for better work?

The actual answer to all of the above questions is definitely "no." Studies show that (perhaps contrary to logic) most employees consider their own work performance to be "above average."

Those judged "above average" by their bosses are merely satisfied, and show no enhanced commitment to their organizations. Those rated "below average" do not become more motivated but rather alienated and demoralized. And those rated "average" or "satisfactory" feel they actually are being unfairly maligned.

This last, and perhaps most surprising, fact was confirmed in a study by Jone L. Pearce and Lyman W. Porter of the University of California, Irvine's Graduate School of Management. They reported that receipt of a low rating (relative to the employee's self-appraisal) caused a distinct and significant drop in attitudes toward the organization within two months of the appraisal. This occurred for both management and non-management employees and persisted even a year later.

For you as a working manager, these findings have important implications. You cannot simply use an appraisal system, expect that it will do what it's supposed to do, and forget it.

To supplement, or perhaps even counteract a formal system, you'll need to take positive steps to increase employee commitment. The more effort you put into managing your employees' work on a day-to-day basis, the fewer the ill effects from a formal appraisal system. Here are some suggestions:

- **Present clear work goals.** The clearer the goals, the more easily you will be able to evaluate performance accurately. In some jobs, numerical goals are appropriate (e.g., "process 75 forms a day" or "sell 100 units a month"), but in others you have to set standards more open to judgment (e.g., "courteous customer assistance" or "frequently demonstrates initiative").

- **Make sure you agree on the goals.** Check that employees understand what you expect of them. Encourage them to restate goals you have set and to ask questions about any facet of the work they feel unsure about.

- **Be consistent.** Don't shift priorities without giving people full and adequate notice. Judge everyone doing similar work by similar standards.

- **Communicate a positive attitude**—about both your own job and theirs. In the Pearce and Porter study, they found that employees' attitudes toward the fairness of the performance appraisal system definitely improved when their managers' attitudes first became more positive.

- **Make evaluation an ongoing process.** The more frequently people get feedback on their work, and the more they trust their supervisor's knowledge of their day-to-day performance, the more they view a formal appraisal as fair and accurate—regardless of the ratings they get.

  It's advisable not to wait for that once- or twice-a-year form to fill out. Instead, let people know what you think of their work as they do it.

- ▪ **Observation:** Formal performance appraisal systems are most useful as periodic summaries of what you have been saying to people informally all along. Then, they are least likely to be resented and most likely to be believed.

Getting the Message Across
Under Fire

— You've called your staff together to explain that more cutbacks will necessitate reassignments and reduced benefits. They vent their frustration with remarks like, "Why didn't we hear about this earlier?" and "How come managers don't have to double up too?"

— You are proposing a campaign to a client's marketing department. They have not forgotten your staff's blunder in the previous campaign and roar disapproval: "You promised that the last time—why should we trust you now?"

— You are presenting a new promotion to the sales force. They interrupt with challenges and criticism. "How do you expect anyone to believe that?" and, "You've got to be kidding if you think I'm going to lug all that sales literature around all day."

Weaving through a landmine of controversy and criticism to make a point is difficult, but not impossible, says Jim Smith, senior vice president for Communispond, Inc., a communications consulting firm in Chicago. He suggests that you:

▪ **Prepare for the worst.** If the information you are conveying is controversial or unwelcome, or if your relationship with the group is already strained, expect to meet objections, hostility or sarcasm. "Plan ahead by putting yourself in the audience's place and imagining how they might respond," advises Smith. Structure your material to address concerns before they are voiced—perhaps with handouts or a chart. Prepare answers to sticky issues that may arise. If the atmosphere is charged when you begin, clear the air at the outset ("We take full responsibility for that error and I promise it won't happen again").

▪ **Take questions only at the end.** This gives you more control of the meeting and prevents you from getting sidetracked. It also enables you to address people's concerns up front, thereby reducing hostility during the question-and-answer period.

- **Avoid sounding defensive or bland.** If you try to prevent attack by defending your position, the audience may feel challenged and could take the offensive.

  People who anticipate pressure often come across as bland; they hide behind a prepared statement or deluge the audience with various facts and figures. "It makes them seem uncaring at a time when people most need sincerity and conviction," explains Smith. "Project sincerity, conviction and naturalness through your voice, animation, eye contact and facial expression."

- **Confront attacks honestly.** How should you respond to an accusing question or a venomous attack? "First, make a statement that acknowledges the person's feelings," says Smith. For example: "I can understand why you are upset." Then repeat or rephrase, and answer the question. This achieves three purposes: It gives you time to decide how to respond; it clarifies or confirms the question or statement; and it helps defuse hostility.

  For example, an employee says: "I think the benefits plan stinks. What's in it for us?" Your response: "It's natural to feel anxious about a major change like this. Let me clarify what this plan means for you." If the employee responds by citing a specific example ("My brother-in-law works in the Toledo branch and he says . . ."), offer to discuss it privately after the meeting.

  "Look beneath the surface for the person's real concern," advises Smith. Don't let yourself be sidetracked by some heated, emotional attacks.

- ■ **Observation:** No matter how much opposition you encounter, it's important to keep your cool so you can control the interaction. Once your attackers verbally get the better of you, you've lost the battle. To prevent this from happening, never lose sight of your goal: to simply, effectively and candidly communicate information that will answer questions and resolve the situation. Then you will always act objectively.

Coping With Employee Resistance

People are going to resist what they don't want. It could be something they find dull, overwhelming, frustrating, boring or threatening in some way.

No matter what the reason, resistance is healthy and ought to be expected. It's good for workers because it allows them to vent feelings, and it's also good for the company because it provides valuable information. But it also poses problems for the manager when work has to be completed.

Strategy: Avoid techniques such as coercion ("It must be done or else"), minimizing the problem ("I'm sure you can find time to get the report finished") or deflection ("Once you see the great results, you'll feel a lot better about the project"). A creative and effective way to deal with resistance is to realize that it is a powerful force in the organization, and then to work with it.

These tips can help:

- **Bring it to the surface.** Don't let it simmer silently. It's not good for the individual, office morale and/or productivity. Find out exactly what the objections are and how strongly they are felt.

- **Explore causes.** Determine origins of resistance and pseudo-resistance. There is a realistic cause behind authentic resistance ("I don't have time to work on this project"), whereas another motive or hidden agenda ("This project is not going to get us anywhere—it's a waste of time") usually lurks behind the pseudo variety.

- **Find answers.** If you're dealing with authentic resistance, help the person overcome the barrier. If the individual feels there isn't enough time, analyze his or her schedule. Restructure responsibilities to free up enough time to get the additional work done. If you're up against pseudo-resistance, find out what's really bothering the person and see what can be done to rectify the problem.

- **Observation:** It's unrealistic to expect to rid yourself of resistance. A practical and feasible goal is to get the resistance down to a manageable level that does not hinder your overall effectiveness.

The Hidden Message:
Leave Us Alone!

— In an attempt to encourage more communication with her staff, a manager institutes a policy of taking a different employee to lunch each week. She also makes it a point to make the rounds every couple of days for informal chats. After a while she finds that employees are canceling their lunch dates. She also discovers that they find her visits intrusive and artificial.

— In order to review the status of ongoing projects, keep everyone informed, and provide a forum where employees can speak their minds, a department head schedules daily 9:00 a.m. meetings. After the first week, attendance declines.

— An administrator who advocates participative management sends employees a detailed questionnaire designed to elicit suggestions for improvement and announces a series of follow-up meetings. Employees respond with an "If it ain't broke, don't fix it" attitude, and their response level is very low.

These managers' efforts to open up communication are actually putting employees off. What might they do differently?

"There is no one correct answer which applies to every manager in every situation," say Kim S. Cameron, associate professor of organizational behavior at the University of Michigan's Graduate School of Business in Ann Arbor, MI. "It depends on the history of the relationship, corporate culture and the time frame in which a manager must produce bottom line results." Cameron describes the pros and cons of various options:

▪ **Reschedule dates and times.** In an effort to get participation, you might change the 9:00 a.m. meetings to 3:00 p.m. or make the lunch dates biweekly. "The positive side of this kind of persistence is that you show that you are really serious—that you're not just following a fad you read about in a management book," explains Cameron. Eventually, employees may see that you mean business and come around to your ways.

119

The negative side is that you may be perceived as a nag. "At the same time that people wish you would disappear, they realize they can't say no to the boss," adds Cameron. "Thus, they engage in secretiveness or avoidance behavior which drains their energy from productivity."

- **Lay down the law.** You might just say, "I'm the boss and it is mandatory that everyone follow my policies." Lee Iacocca was able to carry this off and come out looking like a charismatic, visionary leader, notes Cameron. "If handled well, this approach can rev people up and motivate them to follow your command."

If not communicated in a positive way, however, strong commands can make you seem autocratic and lead to resistance, anger and political subterfuge.

- **Drop the idea altogether.** If it becomes apparent that your plan is not working, you may decide that it just isn't feasible, and let things slip back to the way they were. "This tack can actually work, as long as it is coupled with an alternative," says Cameron. "Make it clear that you are giving up on this particular idea, but that you are not giving up your goal. Then you launch Plan B." This can demonstrate that you are flexible and can enhance, rather than inhibit, group productivity and morale.

On the other hand, you run the risk of placing yourself in a win-lose situation where the employees have won. "This can give the message that you are not strong enough to run your operation, or it may say that you admit to having bad ideas," explains Cameron. "Employees can deduce from this that your future ideas won't be much better." Thus, you lose power, leadership and the much-needed ability to motivate.

- **Ask employees for their ideas.** "Commitment rises markedly when employees are involved in decision making," says Cameron. "When ideas become 'ours' versus 'the boss's,' people's energy rises, too." In addition, you may receive workable suggestions you hadn't thought of yourself.

On the flip side, this tends to be a time-consuming endeavor, and thus a costly one. Also, if employees offer suggestions you reject, you open yourself to criticism for soliciting ideas with no intent of using them. Weigh all of your alternatives carefully, and then make your final decision.

Helping Employees
Through Personal Crises

When someone who works for you suffers a personal misfortune—perhaps a death in the family or a work-related disappointment, such as the loss of a major account—there's a natural urge to sympathize. That urge makes good business sense because it strengthens a humane working relationship and helps the employee to recover.

Sympathy is an emotion that is easy to feel, yet is also most difficult to convey. Consider this advice:

- **Listen carefully.** Let the employee express feelings (anger, sorrow, frustration or disappointment) without being judgmental. Avoid hindsight reflections that focus on "what might have been."

- **Help the person to accept reality.** It may seem comforting to minimize or deny the impact of the trouble. To help the employee come to terms with what has happened, you are in a position to provide a helpful perspective, especially if you have suffered a similar personal crisis, or if the crisis is work-related. However, don't offer hopes that may prove false. There can be nothing more annoying to someone in pain than to be fed optimistic clichés such as: "A month from now you'll see it all in a much clearer light," or "You've got to take hold of yourself."

- **Remind the employee of his or her strengths.** At times of loss, people's self-confidence often flags under stress. As manager, you are in an excellent position to address the employee's personal qualities that can be called on to weather the crisis.

- **Offer specific aid, if possible.** For personal crises, remind the employee of the company's policy for paid time off or extended unpaid leave. If the situation calls for it, review relevant health care benefits. For work-related crises, offer the person assignments, or further training, that can help him or her recover professionally.

- **▪ Observation:** Asking the employee to reveal all the personal details of the trouble, or his or her plans or intentions, can put

121

you in an unwanted guardian's role. Don't push beyond what the employee is willing to volunteer unless it involves business matters for which you intend to take full responsibility. Anything else is both a personal and private matter.

When to Say "I'm The Boss!"

Occasionally, every manager must use his or her authority to take over a difficult situation without explanation or discussion. At such times, pulling rank is not only acceptable, but necessary. Dr. Leland Forst, a vice president at the New York City office of the management consulting firm, A.T. Kearney, suggests scenarios when this arbitrary use of power may be called for:

When you alone can save the day. "Sometimes the manager has information, know-how or authority that the employee lacks," says Forst.

Example: A subordinate is making a presentation to a client group and you see them becoming uneasy or antagonistic. By virtue of your relationship with the client, your knowledge of confidential information, or just your position (people are generally less inclined to challenge a senior person), you can override the employee and steer things back on course.

When you must protect confidentiality. From ignorance, immaturity or a misguided desire to help or impress, a subordinate may expose too much. If you step in quickly and deftly, you can cram the lid back on the can of worms.

When time is running short. With a deadline, time may not permit much more than a "Do it because I said so" directive. Of course, be aware that this is definitely an emergency measure.

When an employee needs coaching. "If you see an employee mishandling a situation, you might take over to demonstrate a better approach," notes Forst.

Example: The employee is getting nowhere with a presentation. You intervene, using a different angle.

It's tricky to pull rank without demeaning your subordinates or eroding their respect for you. Do it only when absolutely necessary and do it gracefully. Some guidelines:

- **Establish an understanding up front.** At the start of a staff relationship, always indicate clearly which rules are totally non-negotiable. Then the employees involved won't be unpleasantly surprised later.

    Example: If you establish that employees are never to discuss one client with another, they won't be mystified when you cut off someone about to breach that confidentiality.

- **Rehearse the cues.** When you foresee the potential need to pull rank, review the protocol with your people so that they can step aside gracefully.

    Example: "If I stand up and interject something while you're presenting, that's your sign to sit down and let me take over."

- **Preserve the employee's dignity.** You can override someone without talking down or being disrespectful.

    Example: When cutting in on the employee who is floundering in a presentation, avoid embarrassing him ("You can sit down now, Al"). Instead, say, "Thank you, Al. You've raised some good points and I'd like to comment further."

- **Follow up.** To avoid misunderstandings or bad feelings, explain to the person your reasons for having pulled rank.

    Example: "I took the reins because you couldn't possibly have known about the latest merger negotiations."

- ■ **Observation:** Pulling rank should be used sparingly. Before stepping in, ask yourself: Am I doing this to feed my ego, or is it for the good of the unit? Then you may act on your honest reply.

Ask Yourself: Are You "Them"?

"*They* want us to do it this way."

"You can't expect any more from *them*."

"*They* will never go along with it."

In the eyes of some employees, every manager becomes, at one time or another, the personification of "them." This happens when workers look upon rules and procedures as mandatory—because you, the executive, decreed them—rather than accept them because they serve a useful purpose.

Aside from the fact that being dubbed "them" hurts your ego, there are more pressing, objective reasons why this employee's frame of mind is destructive. First, it breeds passivity, and that can stultify a work group or a department, and second, it turns much of what ought to be cooperative effort toward common goals into an adversarial situation— the typical "us versus them" frame of mind.

It is easier to prevent this attitude among employees than it is to turn it around once it has taken hold—although it is not impossible to do so. The following steps are sound preventive practice, and can also be used to improve poor morale:

- **Maintain contact.** The more visible and accessible you are, the less chance you have of being the object of distorted impressions from subordinates.

- **Make your philosophy known.** In most cases, you don't have to explain why things have to be done. That's why you've created rules, systems and procedures. But you do have to explain the thinking behind the directives you give.

- **Get their perspective.** The more accessible you become, the more likely people will be to sound off informally to you about their work. This gives you an opportunity to see how things can be changed.

- **Watch out for ruts.** You may find that some of your employees' gripes about existing procedures have merit. When it is in your power to alter rules or systems, express appreciation to those who voiced the need for change. When it's not in your power to make the change, keep people informed about the steps you're taking to accomplish that end. By doing so, you're not only responding to work irritants or bottlenecks, but you're also demonstrating how valuable you consider the people who work for you.

▪ ▪ **Observation:** To run a tight, productive operation, managers must be perceived as human and fallible. That reality will encourage workers to express opinions and feelings. It's imperative that subordinates feel that they have the power to change and improve their situations, thereby benefiting themselves and the company.

Inheriting a Less-Than-Ideal Staff

You have accepted your dream job, only to find, after a couple of months, that you are heading up a department of people you never would have hired yourself. Some are unmotivated, and some have the wrong temperament for the work. Others have troublesome personalities, and the rest appear to be incompetent. Worse yet, it is virtually impossible to terminate or transfer anyone, at least for a while.

Your assessment of the situation is really quite negative. So, under the circumstances, is there anything that you can do to salvage the operation?

"Part of the manager's job is to get employees to be motivated, competent and productive," says Martin M. Broadwell, president of The Center for Management Services, Inc., a consulting firm in Decatur, GA, and author of *Supervising Technical and Professional People* (John Wiley & Sons, 1 Wiley Drive, Somerset, NJ 08873; $29.95). "If a supervisor were not faced with that challenge, an essential part of his or her job would be missing." Broadwell also offers these three basic suggestions:

▪ **Assign a task force.** "People are most likely to respond in solving a problem if they are given a role in creating the solution," advises Broadwell. Call in your staff and explain the nature of the problem, whether it is one of morale, production or skills. Then set a team to work on formulating solutions and assure the members that you will take their suggestions seriously and supply whatever help you can.

- **Individualize the problems.** "When you say, 'Our group has problems,' what you really mean is that the individuals in the group have problems," says Broadwell. It is important, then, to meet separately with each employee. First, explain your perception of how that person's job should be done. Then describe specifically how you perceive the employee's present performance. Next, request the employee's input on how he or she can bring these two perceptions into alignment. Last, list the consequences of the employee's not improving, such as denial of raises or promotions.

- **Provide effective training.** Your staff must be trained in how to motivate, discipline and relate to the people they oversee. Those people, in turn, must be trained in how to perform their work effectively.

  "Ninety-five percent of training is done incorrectly," states Broadwell. "People make the mistake of simply using the show-and-tell method." Instead, he recommends that employees be told and shown what to do and then asked to repeat back, in their own words, what they have learned. Finally, they should demonstrate what they have learned. This process will help the training to sink in and will show the trainer whether employees have really grasped it.

- • **Observation:** Regardless of how unsuitable and hopeless your staff appears, avoid labeling or judging people as deadbeats or incompetents. Begin with the premise that you are going to turn things around and you face a much better chance of success.

A Need for Today: Positive Discipline

"You've been uncooperative, lax and late for work three times in a row. Take tomorrow off—with pay."

Has this supervisor gone dotty, rewarding poor performance with a day off? What's going on?

It's positive discipline at work. The technique, introduced more than 20 years ago by Canadian industrial psychologist John Huberman, has been used at organizations like General Electric, Union Carbide, AT&T, the Texas Department of Mental Health and Mental Retardation, and others.

Punishment Doesn't Work

"Our entire society is based on a criminal justice system that says that crime or misbehavior must be punished," notes Richard C. Grote, former president of Performance Systems Corp. in Dallas, a pioneer in the dissemination of positive discipline. "But as we know, the system doesn't have the desired effect: improved behavior. Furthermore, most employees aren't criminals."

Workers who are punished usually don't become better workers. By contrast, positive discipline has resulted in significant improvements in employee performance, absenteeism and morale.

With nonpunitive discipline, the responsibility for change lies squarely on the employee's shoulders.

A Change of Attitude

It isn't easy to shake off ingrained societal beliefs. Most companies that adopt positive discipline undergo a radical transformation in their attitudes toward discipline, performance and individual responsibility. But even without a company-wide wrenching, an individual manager can begin to apply the tenets of positive discipline.

"First, it's important to acknowledge that you can't really control an employee's behavior—you can only influence it," says Grote. "This realization alone is a great relief because you've shifted the responsibility to where it belongs: the employee. You are no longer the bad guy."

A concrete example is the performance discussion. This always involves excuses. Rather than argue with the employee, you accept the excuse: "Yes, that is a problem" (the car wouldn't start, the baby-sitter didn't show, another department was late with its figures). "How are you going to handle it?" Emphasize responsibilities the person has toward the job.

Implementing Positive Discipline

- **Oral reminder.** Manager and employee meet to discuss a specific performance problem. The object is to gain the employee's agreement to solve it. Rather than issue a warning of more serious discipline to come, the manager reminds the worker of an obligation to meet company standards of behavior. A record of this meeting does not go into the employee's personnel file, but the manager keeps notes for a working file.

- **Written reminder.** This is in order if the problem persists, followed by another meeting to discuss the employee's failure to abide by the original agreement. Again, the manager attempts to get the employee's cooperation. A record of this meeting is placed in the employee's file.

- ■ **Observation:** Under old-style discipline, the employee feels punished and resentful ("I did wrong, they got me for it, I've paid my dues"). Positive discipline is corrective, not punitive. It says to the employee: "You are really responsible for your own actions."

  "This system allows management to stop beating up on people," concludes Grote. "It's a mature way to deal with problems," and one that most employees usually seem to find is quite reasonable.

Can You Be Trusted as a Boss?

Traditional methods for building trust between managers and workers are to stress common objectives, build group spirit, and offer motivational rewards.

But this "shared fate" approach is flawed, contend Samuel Culbert and John J. McDonough, co-authors of *Radical Management: Power Politics and the Pursuit of Trust* (Free Press, 866 Third Ave., New York, NY 10022; $24.95).

"It is impossible to keep redefining every situation so that all employees feel they have the same goal, and it is unrealistic to expect people to continually subordinate their personal interests," says McDonough, a professor of management at UCLA. He has found that real trust grows when employees are consistently shown that their needs are understood and respected.

"Employees will track their boss to see how worthy he or she is of their trust," says McDonough. The acid test:

- **How do you handle criticism from employees?** Managers don't have all the answers, and should encourage skepticism. Trust is built when workers feel comfortable enough to question orders and rules. Even if a criticism is unfounded, it's important that workers know that they can always voice their opinions honestly without suffering any repercussions.

- **Do you respect individual differences?** People differ in their goals, opinions and working style. "Rather than asking them to subordinate these differences for the good of the team, encourage free expression," advises McDonough. The puzzle pieces still fit together into a unit. Any compromises that may be necessary will be made more willingly when people feel that their strengths and feelings are valued.

- **Do you offer support?** Employees are more likely to trust someone who will promote and, if necessary, fight for them.

- **Are you appreciative?** People have more confidence in a boss who values their contributions. If you focus mainly on weaknesses, you risk creating an atmosphere of suspicion. "Indiscriminate praise, however, raises doubts as to the boss's seriousness and fosters mistrust," adds McDonough. Make sure praise is appropriate to the contribution.

■ ■ **Observation:** Trust must be earned, and thus requires time and interaction. It's crucial for building an enduring relationship with your subordinates.

Is a Subordinate After Your Job?

For many managers, it comes as a shock when "trusted subordinates," whose loyalty and devotion have long been taken for granted, reveal themselves as being after their boss's job.

Think about your most trusted subordinate. Does he (or she) want your job? *Chances are he does.* He may be utterly loyal, a staunch friend—but he wants your job. And what about the situation between you and your own boss? Do you want your boss's job? Probably you do.

How, then, you deal with the subordinate who wants your job—and advance your own hopes as well?

First, don't fight ambition. Instead of fearing the desire to move up, take advantage of it to expand your own job to advance your own goals. Give ambitious subordinates assignments that extend them fully. (These may lead them to the conclusion that there is more to what you do than they may have thought.) Help them, too, to direct their ambitious drive into productive channels. This will assure them that they are being given the maximum chance to get ahead. And you will benefit from the most effective use of the talent.

Look up, not down. Come to terms with the fact of your *own* ambition and be candid with yourself about the fact that *you* want to advance as well. The best way of moving into your boss's job is by building a record of solid performance. And one of the best ways of doing that is by getting the most out of subordinates. This means, in turn, recognizing the fact of their ambitions and working with—not against—them to obtain the greatest possible employee productivity.

130

Wherever there is rank and promotion, the way lies open for wishes that call for suppression. Shakespeare's Prince Hal could not, even at his father's sickbed, resist the temptation of trying on the crown.

We are all tempted to "try on the crown." Help employees earn the crown—and you will be doing the same for yourself.

■ ■ **Observation:** There are, of course, times when managers find themselves in the way of subordinates who will resort to foul means to achieve their ends. In this sort of situation, you may have to play rough, not be able to take action that is considered and temperate. Just be sure, though, that you don't find yourself driven to play so rough that you damage your self-image and your image with others in the organization. No matter what the provocation, you still will have to live with yourself and those you care about.

THE POLITICS OF CHANGE

Surviving When Your
Company Is Merged

Mergers can be tough, as any employee who has survived one can testify. James C. Cabrera, president of the outplacement-counseling firm of Drake Beam Morin Inc., in New York City, and contributor to *The Merger/Acquisition Consultant* newsletter, finds that, even for employees who keep their jobs, anxiety remains high. He says that with a merger a new entity suddenly exists which is unfamiliar to everyone. Things are turned upside down, and the three basic things all employees feel entitled to know—what is expected of them, how their performance will be measured and how they will be rewarded—become unanswered questions. For a time—and it may be a long time—there may simply be no answers.

In this sort of reorganization, you and your employees are likely to be left hanging, wondering whether your positions will be eliminated, restructured or combined; whether you will be demoted, promoted or asked to relocate. During the weeks and months when these unknowns hang in the air, the atmosphere can become heavy with paranoia, fear and rumors. Then, as changes begin to be made—all of them beyond your control—anxiety can induce chaos, and productivity goes down, down, down.

Often, though, you can ease the frustration for both yourself and your employees. You can, for example . . .

- **Seek out positives.** While it's natural to resist change, try not to let anxieties blind you to opportunities. For example, if you'll be converting to the other company's automated systems for functions previously done by hand, this may be your chance to develop computer literacy—a valuable skill for the future. At the same time, you'll demonstrate to your boss that you can adapt easily and eagerly—making you an asset when others, because of their resistance, may be a burden. It's also an opportunity to show how you can hold your operation together amid upheaval—a testament to your managerial skills and a good way to increase your value at a time when those at the top may be scrutinizing managers very carefully.

Additionally, the merger may offer the chance to move your career in a different direction. For example, your first exposure to new technologies might spark your interest and lead to a lateral move into, say, information systems or another area which didn't exist before. With other managers being terminated or relocated, the time may be right to take advantage of openings.

Another consideration: If you want to expand more within your present position, post-merger can be the ideal time. With a general restructuring, top management may be more receptive to new ideas, especially if new senior people have come in bringing new philosophies and goals.

- **Use yourself as an example.** It's not uncommon, when two organizations join, for a "them vs. us" attitude to develop. It's fed by a feeling of powerlessness and resentment as good people are terminated, remaining people relocated or demoted, familiar routines disrupted and new management moved in—all without consulting the people whose lives are affected. When, as a consequence, your employees are feeling at the mercy of forces beyond their control, your challenge (and opportunity) is to emphasize the positives.

   Try starting with your own attitude. Avoid dwelling on "the unfairness of it all" and move on to "How can we benefit?" You thus encourage your employees to do likewise. You can lead the way by talking about the advantages of the merger—better benefits, access to new technologies or outside consultants. You can offer incentives, such as more chances for advancement or the possibility of a transfer to an exciting area.

- **Obtain reliable information.** With new changes happening daily, rumors flying and insecurity rife, it's essential to keep communication flowing with your immediate boss. He or she may be preoccupied and neglect to share information. Exercise your persistence. Let your boss know you want to learn about changes when they happen and to understand the implications, too, so you'll know better what's expected of you and how you can contribute. For instance, if you learn that a new corporate goal is to emphasize service over products, you may want to plan a new training program for your sales staff.

- **Demonstrate that you care.** The more information you share with your employees—even if the news is not all good—the more loyalty you will receive while everyone is pulling through the transition. At a time when it may seem that no one higher up cares, you can show that they are important to *you*. Pass along even seemingly small news items as you receive them, such as, "We'll be moving upstairs in two weeks," or "Our paychecks will start coming on Thursdays beginning next month." When imparting news that may be unsettling, emphasize the positive. "Our CEO is being replaced by theirs. I hear he's well-liked and respected," or "We'll be changing over to their billing system. It will take a while to learn, but eventually, it may make life simpler."

- ■ **Observation:** The purpose of a merger is profit, and some operations in an acquired company may be trimmed, others encouraged to grow. Until you see the direction of your operation, it's a good idea to sustain a positive outlook—as long as it makes sense. But if you see it's going down, then there's no need for you or your people to go down with it. You must be prepared to take action for your own well-being.

Being an Outsider in Your Own Company

"Cognitive divergence" describes the situation of a person whose thinking has become so different from the rest of the group that he or she doesn't really fit in. This person is now considered "out of it," an eccentric, a maverick. Some changes that can make you seem like this in your own organization:

- **Your company may have changed since you joined it as a bright young newcomer.** New people with a different management philosophy may have taken over, or the company may have expanded or changed direction as time passed.

- **Times may have changed.** New ideas, new technology may cause a company to change its outlook. Where once it valued those managers who ran production centers or developed new products, now it may save its smiles for its financial or marketing managers. Or, vice versa.

- **Your place in the company may have changed.** Everything that until now has made you outstanding suddenly stops working. The very characteristics which made you stand out for the old executive team may now make you stumble.

- **You may have changed.** As with a married couple, both you and your company may have developed—but in different directions.

In such circumstances, it is easy for the manager's job to go sour, for the good times to stop. Praise comes in increasingly sparser doses; experiences of success grow fewer; prospects for promotion dwindle. Managers previously at the center of things find it hard to get a hearing for their ideas. It's a new ball game now.

Too many managers in this situation think they have no alternative—they must get out. But this is not necessarily so. Here's what you can do:

- **Play by the rules.** Some companies reward freewheeling managers, others those who go by the book. Study closely what wins favor in the eyes of new executives and what elicits a big groan. A planning manager who had been riding to work on a motorcycle, wearing a leather jacket, switched to a business suit and took to driving a grey sedan when a new executive team took over. "This is my protective coloration," he said. "It's hard enough getting your ideas accepted when you're an insider, much less when you're standing on the outside."

- **Take a close look at yourself.** To keep up with the company's new outlook, you may need new skills. Or you may find that your own values have blinded you to legitimate points in the regime's approach. If you make no attempt to see the point of view of executives, you may have yourself to blame for being in limbo.

- **Be so valuable the company can't get along without you.** As Joe McCarthy, once the manager of temperamental Ted Williams, said: "Any manager who can't get along with a .400 hitter has to be crazy." If you produce a greater profit than anyone else, ex-

138

ecutives will not only put up with your eccentricities, they'll learn to love them.

- **Build on your "eccentricities" as the source of your strength.** A healthy organization needs managers who complement each other, not ones who are each other's clones. If you see things differently, you have value to your company as a divergent thinker—the one who sees angles that are invisible to others, possibilities other people haven't thought of. The trick is to present these differing insights as enhancing the position of company executives, not in a way that seems to undermine them.

- **Find a part of the company you match.** In a large enough organization, there's at least one section that most values past experiences; one that prefers innovation; one that needs fast reaction to immediate events; one that requires patient consideration of all the facts. Find your match.

- **Wait them out.** Let your bosses get better acquainted with how you operate and what results you get. If your views have been right all along, the message should get through. If despite your opinions the company has flourished, that should give you something to think about too.

- ▪ **Observation:** In the end, you've got to be you. You will do best as a manager in an organization whose ways you accept and where you act in ways that are natural to you and not put on. But going to another organization is not a move that any manager makes lightly—certainly not before he or she has explored the options his or her own company has to offer.

Transition From Power
as You Grow Older

Even in an era where mandatory retirement ages are creeping higher and higher, corporate managers need to plan for their own transitions from the seat of power to new roles and other activities.

For some, a top consideration is perpetuating a philosophy of business that they feel they have helped their companies develop. They want to

139

know that what they have contributed to the corporate culture and success will not be lost.

Others are more pragmatic. They accept that new management must set its own standards and tone. They put their energies into planning for their own futures elsewhere.

There are many managers who don't care too deeply about what happens to their organizations after they leave. Such managers recognize that corporations are, by their nature, designed to survive the individual employee, and they, therefore, see little value in staying too emotionally involved.

But any lack of concern you may feel after you're gone is not quite the same as what you might feel while you're still in command, yet with the end in sight. Advises a Florida manager who is in this category: "One must recognize the deleterious effects of the aging process and plan ahead for the change in command. This plan—to gradually loosen the reins—should be implemented many years before it becomes necessary to turn things over to your successor."

What worries this manager, and others, is that the ego-gratifying, on-top-of-it-all role they now have in their organization will be eroded. You find yourself not advised of certain projects, not informed of certain meetings, listened to not quite so closely, not quite as persuasive as you used to be. Worse, you may find there is little you can do about it. Somehow, the decision has been made, the process set in motion without any conscious action on your part.

Let's assume the above possibility looks pretty dismal to you. That is, retirement is still a few years away, and you'd like to be sure that you lose nothing while you're still Number One in your operation. You'd also like to have some options after you step down. Are there some precautions you might take to be sure that will happen? Here's some counsel that might prove helpful:

- **Hang on to your vigor.** Though age does take its insidious toll, "old" is more a matter of attitude than of actuality. If you maintain your accustomed pace (remain as active as you ever were), then those around you are less likely to pick up signals that could work against you. By the same token, you yourself are less likely to pick up negative signals if your attitude toward continued activity remains as positive as it ever was.

- **Keep your viewpoint progressive.** If managers are seen as obstacles to younger managers in the organization because they represent an outmoded viewpoint, then the process of easing out will probably begin sooner. Youth—like it or not—will be served. So, if you want to avoid the behind-the-back smirks, the head shakes, the tones of voice that convey more than words, you'd do best to concentrate as hard as possible on what is happening right now, rather than on the events and lessons of your long years of experience. Your experience is an asset, but only if you can make it relevant to today's new problems.

- **Mind the store.** While it's tempting to think that, since you've paid your dues, you're entitled to some rest and recreation while others do the work, this is also dangerous. Much can happen while you're on an extended vacation or away from your desk for long, unaccounted-for periods. Your disengagement will be observed, noted and eventually become part of a negative equation by which you are judged. If you want to stay on top of the business, you have to be there physically and mentally.

- **Stay oriented.** You can't really afford to let changes occur that do not have your concurrence—even those that are relatively small. "I learned that I hadn't been given a copy of an interim report on a new product," notes a manager in his sixties. "I immediately made a phone call and made damned sure that wasn't going to happen again." If you still have important contributions to make, be sure they are heard.

- **Take on new activities, other roles.** The more useful you are to your organization, the less likely you are to be discarded. Thus, as a senior executive, it would pay to go after whatever opportunity there may be in your bailiwick to expand your political and community contacts. If you're seen as having the ability to extend your organization's influence, help it reach its objectives without political interference and enable it to stay out of trouble, then it's likely you will continue to be valued. You probably have important outside contacts that are very useful to your company. Keep them alive.

- **Stay political within the organization.** Success in a corporate setting is often as much a product of personal relationships as of native talent or ability. Whether or not this is true in your case, it can still be important—even essential—to keep your relationships as warm as possible with those who have helped you in the past and who could help you in the future. Keep up with the people you have mentored over the years.

- **Consider your successor.** By now, you should have established a solid, over-the-years relationship with a younger manager who is clearly perceived as being the logical candidate to succeed you. If you haven't, then there is no time to waste. Your objective: the career development of someone who will implement not only what is good for the organization but also what is good for you. A tall order, perhaps, but worth exploring.

- **Observation:** It's only realistic to assume that there are ambitious people in your operation who want—and perhaps deserve—the power, pay and prestige that your position commands. Their desire to see you go may have less to do with their personal opinion of you than with their own needs. They may also be influential with those who control your span of office. About the only way you can deal with this sort of pressure is to plan as carefully as possible, try to be as unique and irreplaceable as you know how—and then, with grace and dignity, head out under your own timetable with your worthwhile plans for the future.

If Employed by a Corporation, Be Realistic

A network documentary once showed in poignant detail how forced separation from the companies to which they had devoted their most productive years had affected several managers. For some, the effect was disastrous—a loss of confidence, of identity, even of belief in the system that could permit this to happen. Each had worked hard and well for his or her company. "How could they do this to *me?*" was the question that each, in his or her own way, asked.

One response to this question was given by Lord Edward Thurlow, an English jurist and statesman of the 18th century who asked, "Did you ever expect a corporation to have a conscience, when it has no soul to be damned, and no body to be kicked?"

While it is true that corporations work best when they appreciate the human potential of their employees, it is also true that people are, on the corporate books, a cost variable of paramount importance. Without the ability to control such costs, no corporation could survive. And though the managers of some corporations do it more gracefully or logically than others, in the end, the necessity to maintain itself in the marketplace by controlling the size and cost of its work force is an essential function of *all* corporations.

These days—in a lean and mean economic environment—many managers are feeling the cold shadow of the corporate axe. Unfortunately, there is little reason to feel that this threat will disappear. Many personnel experts feel that the days when management ranks were the last to be depleted in a work force cutback are permanently over. Managers are now considered, by and large, as vulnerable as anyone else to either being fired or forced into premature retirement.

One personnel expert, Ray Wicklander, management director for Continental Capital Management Corp., Chicago, says this about those who fail to measure up: "Employees who have hit a plateau in today's economy become an especially difficult burden. We're now competing with the likes of Sears and Merrill Lynch, so we frankly can't afford people with only one trick in their bag, and an old one at that. We don't owe them a living."

Is there anything that you can do about this ongoing process? The answer is yes—provided you are willing to cast loose from any conviction you may have that you deserve total job security from the corporation that employs you. Are you able to . . .

. . . take an unsentimental look at what is happening? Is your corporation forced to fight hard for its share of the market? How have recent events affected its net earnings? What are its prospects? What is happening with similar operations? How are their work forces affected? Have new officers and/or consultants been brought in to bring about changes? How vital is your operation in the corporate scheme of things?

Even if your corporation is making money, and even if your operation seems to be making an intrinsic contribution to the bottom line, there is still good reason to feel insecure. Other operations within the corporation may be ailing, may need shoring up. Your operation, *because* it is doing well, may be viewed by higher management as one whose budget and staff can be safely pared so that scarce financial resources can be shifted.

. . . take a hard look at your job? Are you getting paid a relatively substantial salary? How much would the operation suffer if you were replaced by someone who could be paid substantially less? How much would the operation suffer if your job were to be eliminated altogether, or combined with another job? What would happen to you if your boss were transferred or fired?

Many especially conscientious managers come to have an unrealistic view of their importance to the corporate scheme of things. They feel that the hard work and long hours they put into getting the job done will be recognized and rewarded, and that each year of this continuing effort makes them all the more valuable. Unfortunately, CEOs or management consultants may not always see it that way.

. . . visualize where you'd be if your job or operation were eliminated? Is there a place for you elsewhere in the company? Do you have a powerful sponsor who could assure you of such a place (and just how powerful is this sponsor)? Would you accept a geographical transfer? A substantial pay reduction? Sharply differing duties? A position with lessened responsibilities? Could you get a similar job elsewhere in your field? Could you enter another field or go into business for yourself? Could you happily handle retirement at this point in your life?

Job-Hunting Strategies
for Managers Over 50

Despite laws and company policies prohibiting age discrimination, employers are sometimes unwilling to hire older managers or even consider interviewing them. They erroneously believe that experienced managers are too costly, too set in their ways or too inflexible to work well in today's lean and mean business environment.

If you're unhappy in your present job or suspect that you will soon be in the job market, however, don't allow the possibility of prejudice to negatively influence your efforts to find a position. Plenty of employers are looking for experienced professionals. It's up to you to convince them that you're a good catch. Here are some pointers to follow:

- **Take the buffet approach to looking for a job.** Start by asking those who know you and your work to make introductory calls on your behalf to potential employers they know personally. Recommendations can go a long way towards your being seriously considered. You may have to swallow your pride to ask this favor, but it's worth it if the person thinks highly of you and is in a position to help.

Beyond that, try executive search firms, respond to help-wanted ads and contact employers directly. Even if one or more of these methods hasn't worked for you in the past, it may this time around. The more feelers you put out, the better your chances are.

- **Show your flexibility.** Depending on how much difficulty you're experiencing, it may be to your advantage to indicate in a cover letter or in an interview your willingness to be an individual contributor (rather than a manager), work for someone who is younger than you, take a job that may be considered a lateral or downward move or accept a cut in pay. It's important to address these issues even if the employer doesn't bring them up. Otherwise the employer (particularly if he or she is younger than you) may make some incorrect assumptions.

- **Demonstrate your willingness to be a team player.** Another common employer prejudice is that senior managers are looking for a cushy preretirement position. It's in your best interest to communicate your enthusiasm for working hard. Cite examples of how you met deadlines, contributed to the success of a project, or otherwise made a difference in productivity. Show that you are making a definite contribution.

- **Avoid criticizing your current employer.** Even if you resent the way you're being treated, you can't afford to let prospective employers think you're a complainer or a prima donna. You want to show that, as a mature professional, you've risen above this kind of attitude.

- **Consider registering with a temporary agency.** More agencies are placing professionals with experience into staff positions (which are often the targets of downsizing). Employers don't apply the same tough standards to temporary employees. Once you're ''in,'' you can prove your worth, which may result in the permanent job offer you're seeking. It's an indirect route that can prove to be very effective.

MANAGING DIFFICULT EMPLOYEES

Dealing With the Dissenter

In any group of employees, you're bound to find some who don't hesitate to speak their minds, even if their opinions are unpopular.

This is not inherently good or bad. But you need to learn to distinguish between well-intentioned objections, which contain valid insights, and ill-meant dissent, which tends only to stir up conflict. You must find a place for the former and authority to defuse the latter. Some suggestions:

- **Look for patterns.** Not everyone who states a divergent viewpoint is really trying to cause trouble in the workplace. "Employees tend to build histories of conduct based on consistent intentions," observes Dr. Ralph H. Kilmann, a professor of business administration at the University of Pittsburgh and author of *Beyond The Quick Fix* (Jossey-Bass Publishing, 350 Sansome St., San Francisco, CA 94104; $25.95). "When someone establishes a track record for taking issue with company policy, that record usually shows a pattern in the way it is expressed. It is not difficult to detect the person's intent through the mode of expression."

  If you see that a person tends to come down hard and strong on company policy, but offers reasonable alternatives and avoids personal attacks, it will be clear that the intent was positive. But if someone repeatedly creates animosity by lying, harassing and accusing, it will become obvious that the intent is not to help the organization but rather to achieve some personal gain.

  The only effective way to deal with this kind of person, says Kilmann, is to issue a strong statement warning the employee that such behavior will not be tolerated.

- **Steer employees' objections in the right direction.** Certain corporate cultures frown on dissent, however constructive it might be. This need not prevent you from encouraging it within your unit. Just be sure that employees know when and where it is appropriate

149

to speak up, because this is an important skill for them to possess. "Impress on your people the importance of presenting a united front outside of your department," advises Kilmann. "Rather than telling them to suppress their opinions, explain that it could damage the unit if certain outsiders were to perceive disagreement within your group."

Help your people to recognize those who value dissent and the others who see all disagreement with authority as a destructive element. This will aid them in developing the sophistication that is needed for complaining constructively to the right people.

Coping With the Poor Performer

When an employee's job performance is poor, few managers want to consider dismissal as the first option. For economic, legal and societal reasons, substandard work should be seen as an opportunity for positive managerial intervention.

To boost performance, you must find the cause of the failure and then work with the employee to overcome it. To analyze the situation, consider these questions:

- **Is the problem temporary?** If a competent employee suddenly falls down on the job, there may be temporary, external reasons. Perhaps he or she is not well, or is going through a personal crisis. Or, perhaps there is a short-term change in the work—say, a sudden overload, or a particularly taxing assignment. Find out what the problem is, and offer moral support and substantive help. Encourage the employee to keep you informed about the progress of the problem, and try temporarily to lighten the workload, if it is at all possible.

- **Can the person do the job?** This is the first question to ask about either a new employee or someone new to a particular kind of work. Does he or she have the right experience? What about interest level and appropriate personal traits?

    You may discover that certain skills are lacking. If so, offer training opportunities. Or, you may find that the person and the task are simply mismatched. You should switch the employee to more compatible work.

- **Does he or she know what's expected?** Sometimes, employees don't understand how the work is to be performed and what results are expected. Sit down with the employee and discuss the nuts and bolts of the job and how the individual feels about it. This will help you identify and clarify areas of uncertainty.

- **Does the employee get appropriate feedback?** Sometimes, poor work comes from your neglect—employees feel that no one else notices or appreciates their work.

   Consider: Does the employee have enough contact with you? Do you offer rewards, incentives and praise when the job is well done?

   If poor communication is the problem, try to oversee the employee's work more regularly, so that constructive criticism can be given.

- • **Observation:** Most poor performers will respond quickly and gratefully when you take the appropriate steps to help them improve their performance. Once things are going well, make a point of demonstrating your continuing support, interest and appreciation—and you'll avoid relapses.

A Sniper Can Hurt Your Operation

Your office manager is really furious. He's just found out that the bookkeeper has been making insulting remarks about him behind his back. "Ever since I became her supervisor, she's resented me—probably because I don't let her get away with sloppy work. But I really think this is outrageous. What are you going to do about it?"

Here is one of those situations you wish would go away by itself. Personality clashes do occur and sometimes straighten themselves out with time. But this one seems to call for your intervention.

Here are some steps you might take:

- **Verify the incident.** When a report reaches you third-hand, you need to confront the source: "It's come to my attention that you've been making insulting remarks about your supervisor behind his back. Is this true?''

- **Explain the consequences.** Say the individual admits to the charge. She may dispute the details (''I didn't really call him an opportunist—I just said he was ambitious''). Point out that malicious gossip usually hurts others and undermines the effectiveness of the department.

- **Request an apology.** Explain that the person who has been maligned would be within his rights to file an official complaint. This would leave the gossiper in danger of disciplinary action. Should an apology then be made, note it in a memo with copies to both parties.

- **Keep tabs on the situation.** An apology is only the beginning. Try to determine if the employee's antisocial behavior is still a problem. If it is clear that she wastes time and is uncooperative, then let her know that she is on warning for poor performance.

- **▪ Observation:** By giving the employee a chance to make amends, you've demonstrated your fair-mindedness to all of your staff. You've also shown them that the well-being of the department comes first. The offender will either have to change or risk dismissal for cause, since things are now out in the open.

Handling the Hostile Employee

Snide remarks, sullen silences, cynical jokes, rude behavior, and a generally uncooperative attitude. These are a few common characteristics of an employee who has a chip on his shoulder.

This kind of behavior is often tolerated because the employee does make an important contribution to your organization. At times, he can even be agreeable and pleasant. If he has been this way for years, co-workers have probably learned to live with his quirky personality—if nothing else, it gives them something to talk about.

A problem arises if co-workers and/or customers are complaining. Without doing anything hasty, you need to determine why the person's negative behavior has intensified.

- **Discuss the problem.** Speak to the person in a neutral setting. Describe specific incidents representative of the behavior you find disturbing. For example, "When I asked you for the sales figures, you said, 'I told you they're not ready yet,' " or, "Customers report that you sometimes hang up abruptly without saying goodbye."

  Use nonaccusatory language and focus on behavior. After describing the incidents, encourage the person to talk about them. For example, You might say 'I was puzzled by your behavior. Perhaps you can explain.'

- **Listen closely.** If it's clear that you aren't trying to pass judgment on the employee, that you are truly seeking the facts, the person may open up. Even if he rambles or makes excuses, there may be clues in what he says. Perhaps he resents changes made in procedures, or maybe he feels slighted because he wasn't given an adequate raise or promotion. Or there may be personal pressures at home that are making him more hostile than usual.

- **Describe consequences.** In a firm but dispassionate way, remind the employee that there are certain standards of conduct expected of everyone regardless of personal feelings or pressures. Point out that when these norms are not followed, customers get upset, teamwork is hampered, and productivity suffers.

  Furthermore, you can show that appropriate behavior has a direct effect on employee evaluations, promotions, raises and even terminations.

- **Follow up.** This may mean a meeting in two weeks to review progress and give a word of praise to reinforce the new behavior. To the employee, this communicates your concern and awareness of what is going on.

- ▪ **Observation:** Chances are the employee is not very happy as the company curmudgeon and might welcome your intercession. But if he really can't help himself, then you need to decide whether professional help is called for or if a less public job is in order for this particular employee because of his unusual personality.

When a Promotion You Made Fizzles

Sometimes you elevate a staff member only to discover that the person is not up to snuff. In over his or her head, the newly promoted employee can slow the output of your department, unsettle customer relations, or call your judgment into question.

Letting the employee go may be a quick way of handling the problem and saving face, but it can hurt your standing with the rest of your staff, particularly if the person was a good performer in the past. Here are some alternate strategies:

- **Be on the lookout for potential trouble.** ''During the initial honeymoon period, managers often overlook the person's shortcomings, but doing so means mistakes can reach even greater proportions before they're caught,'' says Dr. Chester Schriesheim, distinguished professor of management and the Rosa R. and Carlos M. de la Cruz scholar in leadership at the University of Miami School of Business Administration.

   If external measures of a person's performance are applicable (e.g., sales quotas, weekly reports), review them from the start. Also, tune in to complaints from customers, colleagues and subordinates who are often in a good position to judge how well the recently promoted person is faring.

- **Diagnose the problem.** Once you spot the symptoms, assess how serious the person's mistakes or shortcomings are. If they're disrupting the flow of work or are likely to cause a major crisis if they're not dealt with, take action immediately. If they're what you would expect given the employee's experience and the demands of the new job (e.g., unpolished but thorough reports), allow the person time to grow into all the new responsibilities to be faced.

- **Discuss the situation with the promoted employee.** If performance isn't up to par, the individual is probably aware of it and very possibly worried about it. Ask whether he or she agrees with your assessment of the situation. You might ask for the employee's

154

suggestions on what should be done. Once you've pinpointed the difficulties, consider these options:

- **Try additional training.** The employee may be able to improve performance with formal or informal help. Look into courses your company offers, or have the employee investigate off-site classes or seminars. Another possibility is to have the person work with a more experienced staff member for a while.

- **Take the person under your wing.** If the decisions your staff member is being asked to make are important ones, you might ask for his or her recommendations, but reserve final approval for yourself. Explain why you agree or disagree with the individual's analysis of the situation. This alternative can be time-consuming, but it's the price you may have to pay to save a premature promotion. Once the employee learns what goes into a sound decision, you can then relinquish your mentoring role.

- **Restructure the job.** If training or mentoring are too costly or time-consuming, you can reconsider the person's job responsibilities. The employee may even be glad that you're relieving him or her of overwhelming responsibilities. The trick is finding another staff member who has the time and inclination to take over the problem areas.

- **Make a lateral transfer.** Asking the person to go back to his or her old job—in effect to give up the promotion—usually isn't the best solution. A face-saving alternative is a transfer to a different job that will make use of the individual's already proven skills.

- - **Observation:** The best way to avoid promotion fizzle is to do your homework before you elevate a staff member. Better yet, have the employee take on the key tasks of the new position on a trial basis before you make your final decision. It's good preparation for the future.

The Employee Who
Goes Over Your Head

You have been aware of the situation for some time now. Bits and pieces of overheard conversations, some rather telling comments from your boss, cryptic glances from some employees. Putting it all together, it seems to add up to one thing: One or more of the people who report to you are going behind your back, taking ideas, complaints, whatever, directly to your boss while bypassing you.

But though you are aware of *what* is happening, you don't know *why* it is. "And that's something I'm going to have to find out," you tell yourself. "I'm getting it from both sides—and I have to find a way to put an end to it." Now you wonder, just what is the best approach to take in a situation of this kind?

No Hasty Moves. So far, you have realized an important truth for managers—the need to deal with an upsetting and potentially dangerous situation. Failure to do so could undermine your position in the organization and eventually erode your authority. But, whatever your present situation may be, it would not be wise to do anything hastily. You might say or do something ineffectual that you would regret later. Rather, you—or any manager in a similar position—would do well to take time first to answer, as objectively as possible, these two very important questions . . .

1. **What kind of relationship do you presently have with your boss?** Many people make the mistake of thinking that any working relationship—be it with a boss, a colleague, a subordinate—continues on an even keel. If it was good yesterday, it must also be good today. But most such relationships veer in different directions from time to time—from good to bad to better, depending on people and circumstances.

   It could be, therefore, that the relationship between you and your boss isn't what you thought it was. It could be that you have done something to cause anger. Or, it could be that there is a kind of power play involved—your boss may actually be encouraging people to come directly to her (or him) in an attempt to gain more power, possibly do you in. Thinking over the situation may reveal some problems that you hadn't even realized existed.

2. **What kind of relationship do you presently have with the people who report to you?** There has to be some reason why people circumvent their immediate bosses. Sometimes, of course, it may be just a ploy to ingratiate themselves with top management. More often, though, it's due to the subordinates' beliefs that their bosses don't want to listen to their ideas, don't want to hear their complaints, don't want to be concerned with their problems—perhaps, because they haven't the power to do anything about them.

Are you open with the people who report to you—and do they feel that they can be honest with you? Are you willing to do something about complaints and provide assistance with problems? Do you encourage people to come to you with ideas and suggestions? In analyzing the situation—again, as objectively as possible—you may find that you have been raising barriers between yourself and the people who report to you. Not intentionally, perhaps, but nonetheless the barriers are there.

Stepping Forward. In line with your evaluation of the situation, you may then want to take the following steps . . .

- **Get on a better footing with your boss.** This will call for some decisive action on your part—you can't expect your boss to make the first move. Make it a point to consult him or her on special problems. Discuss some of your ideas. Ask for backing on a project you would like to undertake. Do all this in person—and do it in an open, friendly manner.

Should you discuss the fact that certain employees have been going behind your back? Probably not at first. But as your working relationship improves, you might bring it up and conclude: "I'd appreciate it if, when something like that occurs again, you would simply refer that person back to me."

- **In the meantime, encourage people to come to you.** This may take some doing at first, particularly if you have fallen into the habit of shutting people off—or out. You might start by calling people into your office to talk over a problem—and you might stop by their offices to discuss ideas. Your aim should be to make them feel that your door is open and your mind is receptive to their

157

thinking. Equally important, you must be ready to act on that thinking, when appropriate—be it in dealing with a complaint, pushing for a solution to a problem, or putting good ideas to immediate use.

When people come to realize that you are indeed in charge, ready and willing to hear them out, it's very likely that they will see no further reason for going around you to get to your boss. They'll see you as the boss—as someone who is both effective and always ready to listen.

When You Face Jealous Peers

Jim Welbach is feeling a bit frustrated these days. He has managed to find room in his budget to hire one extra person in his marketing operation, which means that he has been able to promote one of his staffers, Jane Loudin, to the post of Assistant Marketing Director—on a provisional basis. She will now oversee much of the advertising copy and press releases that Welbach formerly supervised—thus freeing him up for larger projects with his boss, the company's executive VP.

It all sounds reasonable and workable, but like so many plans that look good on an organizational chart, this one has run into a few snags. It seems that the staffers who now write the ad copy and press releases, and who were not offered the job, are not acting in a cooperative fashion with their new supervisor. There are disagreements, arguments about work, the content of the copy, whose ideas get precedence and imagined or not-so-imagined slights, followed by recriminations.

Much more than he had anticipated, Welbach is appealed to by staffers to resolve the conflict. Invariably, then, he finds himself involved. Now, Welbach has begun to suspect that unless he takes measures, he'll be unable to free himself from these new demands that are being made on his time, and will be right back where he started. But he isn't sure about what measures to take.

If you are contemplating the promotion of a staff member to a supervisory position, you may encounter a problem similar to Jim Welbach's—particularly if others on your staff either wanted the promotion themselves, or don't feel the promoted person deserved it. There's a good chance it will take more than your announcement to produce good results. Here's what you might plan on doing *after* you've made your choice:

- **Support your own decision.** Provisional promotions have a built-in weakness—they present the possibility that the person you've decided to promote is, in effect, only a candidate. This, in turn, implies that the group that is being supervised can put their stamp of disapproval on your choice. Thus, certain disgruntled group members who have been passed over are encouraged to engage in adverse lobbying, rather than in trying to cooperate. Your best bet, if your decision is for a trial run, is to keep the arrangement confidential between you and the candidate.

- **Talk to key staffers,** especially those who may think you should have offered the job to them first. You don't have to justify your choice, but you ought to make it clear that it was made only after due consideration. Talk about why you promoted from within instead of bringing in an outside person ("I wanted someone who was qualified and who already knew the operation"). Mention how important it is to you to have the new supervisor supported by people like the person to whom you're speaking.

- **Provide continuing support.** With or without a firm appointment, there will still be those who will assume that your decision can be rescinded if the person you've chosen can be made to look bad. They may, thus, go out of their way to cause difficulties—perhaps not so much because they wanted the job, but because they did not want a peer to get it. It is at this point that you, the manager, have to make it clear that you have stepped aside, that all decisions related to the area over your appointed person's responsibility are his or hers to make.

- **Stay out of arguments.** If you are still, apparently, an arbitrator, then everyone—your appointee included—will assume that you are still making the decisions, and that nothing is final until you have decided that it is. You will thus be perpetuating—even aggravating—the situation you wanted to avoid. Instead of shifting your responsibility onto someone else's shoulders, you have retained it. At some point, you're going to have to say, "Now, I'm out of it."

- - **Observation:** Some managers don't altogether accept the process of letting go when it comes to their own authority. They become worried about what might happen if a promoted subordinate acts independently. Sometimes, an unconscious sabotage takes place—one that undermines their own best interests. The point to remember, once you've made the promotion, is that the process of establishing authority is a very delicate and difficult one. Without your patience, tact and visible support, it's not likely to happen in your department either as quickly or effectively as it should.

Making Room for the Promising Rookie

You have a subordinate who you feel has the makings of greatness. If developed and encouraged, this person could climb to the very top. But with a department or division to run, plus your own responsibilities, it's not always that easy to give your potential star the support and encouragement that's needed. It's a universal problem most managers have to contend with.

Some managers think that talent will win out in the end and that nothing need be done to help promising rookies along. With luck and initiative, they'll make their talents known eventually.

There is some validity to this contention, yet many experts—like James Clawson, an associate professor at the Colgate Darden School of Business Administration at the University of Virginia—feel that managers ought to take an active role in helping subordinates make their mark.

It can make managers look good and help the organization, not to mention bringing the special feeling that accompanies giving a deserving individual the chance to realize his or her potential.

Yet, by assisting a capable subordinate, many managers fear being accused of favoritism. "It's not an issue if you deal with all subordinates fairly," Clawsen says. Teach all of them the fundamentals and be accessible to anyone who needs guidance. If everyone starts out in the same place, the leaders in the pack will soon take the initiative and come to the fore. They'll use their special abilities and eagerness to learn, excel and work just a little harder.

Once promising rookies are spotted, don't be timid about taking them under your wing.

160

What do these talented people need and what part should you play in their development? Clawsen suggests:

- **Active coaching and teaching.** Managers have a dual role: to supervise and teach. The crucial part of the job, according to Clawsen, is teaching. It should be done consciously and diligently. It's important that managers recognize their role as teachers so they devote time and energy to the task. Teaching is a lot harder than most people realize until they do it. It requires understanding, patience, practice and dedication.

- **Respect.** Respect is a two-way street. Ideally, the manager ought to respect and admire the rookie's intelligence, drive and ambition. At the same time, the rookie ought to respect the manager's unique position of having the skills and talent needed to supervise part of the organization and also be a teacher and mentor.

- **Trust.** "If subordinates feel that the boss has his or her best interests at heart, they'll profit from the relationship," Clawsen adds. Mutual trust also leads to an open, friendly and honest rapport, which translates into greater motivation and higher productivity.

- - **Observation:** Once the manager's job is completed and the promising rookie has learned all he or she can, the manager can take some well-deserved pride in knowing that pertinent teaching skills have been inculcated in the rookie as well. It won't be long before the talented person takes what has been learned from you and passes it on to others. The teaching process goes on as the next generation of managers learns the ropes and rises in the company, following the lead of those who have gone before them.

Living With the Whistle-Blower

Whistle-blowers—employees who believe their organizations are engaged in illegal, dangerous or unethical conduct and speak out about it—occupy a peculiar niche in America. On the one hand, the public applauds their courage. On the other, it stands quietly by as the whistle-blowers are punished and ostracized for their revelations.

- Allan McDonald and Roger Boisjoly, engineers at Morton Thiokol, testified about serious technical flaws in the space shuttle *Challenger* and were promptly transferred to menial jobs.
- Herbert Rosenblum, an official of New York's Human Resources Administration, revealed that 14,000 people who had died or moved away were still on the city's Medicaid rolls. His reward: demotion and a pay cut.
- Several years ago, Charles Atchison, a quality control engineer at a Texas nuclear power plant, brought numerous safety infractions to the attention of a regulatory board. He was fired and blackballed.

Whistle-blowers almost inevitably pay a heavy price for breaking what Myron Glazer, a Smith College sociology professor, calls "the unwritten law of social regulations. They break a norm—the norm of loyalty."

They Still Keep Standing Up

Bill Bush, a retired NASA worker and ex-whistle-blower, keeps a computer file on whistle-blowers that has ballooned to 8,500 entries. "In the last 10 years," he says, "my sense is there's been a dramatic increase in whistle-blowing."

Why so many more? Andrew Hacker, a professor of political science at New York's Queens College, feels this is due to the rising education level. People are more professional in their pursuit of the good life: "They wish to believe they are advancing justice, benefiting society, and remaining true to their conscience," even if it means being less than completely loyal to their employers. For many of us today, this has now became a matter of priorities.

Corporate Attitudes Are Changing

It's no secret that high-ranking managers in government and industry have had little use for those they considered snitches in their midst. But in an era when headlines scream every day with stories of payoffs, illegal arms shipments, insider trading and drug smuggling, there is an increasing awareness that management needs all the help it can get in policing its operations.

Some of America's largest and most profitable companies have developed internal mechanisms to deal with potential whistle-blowers.

162

Control Data, Singer and McDonald's created ombudsman programs that appoint a single individual to receive, investigate, and respond to employee complaints. Citibank channels employee complaints through a Committee on Good Corporate Practice, which decides whether the committee will investigate the complaint or forward it up the line. IBM has a Speak Up program which permits its employees to voice complaints and get a response, all with a firm guarantee of anonymity.

In short, well-managed companies are encouraging the honest and concerned employee to blow the whistle on illegalities and malpractices. Through a variety of programs, they provide the whistle-blower with access to people who can correct matters, and they assure protection from reprisal.

How Can You Handle Whistle-blowing?

Supervisors and managers at every level of an organization should be alert to the sudden appearance of a troubled employee, whistle in hand. If your organization has an established procedure for handling employee complaints, be thoroughly familiar with it. If you must act on your own, here are some guidelines from the experts:

- **Help the employee define exactly what he or she is protesting.** Is the alleged situation clearly illegal or dangerous? If it is, your options narrow to a course of quickly establishing facts and taking action. If the employee appears to be simply a critic of a perfectly lawful policy, you can help by warning of dangerous waters ahead. A clumsy complainer may soon be on the street.

- **Be as objective and painstaking as possible in helping the employee assess the validity of the facts.** Can the company's wrongdoing be documented in a way that would persuade a skeptical reporter or judge? Does the protester know all the facts and the relevant laws that are known to management?

- **If your company cannot guarantee job protection for the whistle-blower, put the probable consequences on the table.** Ernest Fitzgerald is a legendary figure in whistle-blowing lore since he took on the Air Force for huge cost overruns on a Lockheed cargo plane. He told *The New York Times* that he gets ten calls a week from potential whistle-blowers. He advises them to think very hard

163

before picking up a whistle, for he likens the action to "setting your hair on fire publicly." One current study says that nine out of ten whistle-blowers still lose their jobs.

■ ■ **Observation:** American society needs people ready to blow the whistle on wrong-doing, and corporate management needs them too. But not too many employees are willing to commit career suicide in the name of truth and justice. IBM's Speak Up program and its guarantee of anonymity is a promising program. The present discrimination against sincere whistle-blowers ought to be countered by responsible businesspeople whenever it appears.